How Write Ads That $ell

23 Ad Executives
Share Their SECRETS for Creating Advertising That Will Get Attention, Win Over Customers, and Make Money

KEY IDEAS on:

Copy • Creative Thinking • Layout • Media
Marketing • Merchandising • Outdoor
Packaging • Production • Retailing
Research • Sales Promotion

Plus a profile of successful work-habits.

How to Write Ads That Sell

23 Ad Executives Share Their Secrets for Creating Advertising That Will Get Attention, Win Over Customers, and Make Money

Published by

Classic Business Bookshelf

Contact info:

KRE Book Group
PO Box 121135
Nashville, TN 37212

For more information on
this series, please visit us
on the web at

ClassicBusinessBookshelf.com

Originally published as 460 Secrets of Advertising Executives

Dee 2017

Table of Contents
ഇ൫

Dedication to
You . . . the Reader

I t is a privilege for the co-authors to dedicate this book to the new generation of keen, eager, young people just entering the fields of advertising . . . marketing . . . public relations . . . and research.

It is hoped that this volume of experiences from the old-timers will kindle fresh enthusiasms in the new-timers.

After those dull or troubled days, when it seems you have done nothing but "shovel smoke" pick up this book. Read the lessons learned and passed on by the old pros. Chances are you will find two or three ideas which will make your tomorrow more interesting and more resultful.

The Authors

Why This Book Was Written

The problem of training is of vital importance in many fields. It is especially acute in advertising and its related crafts. That is because the ratio of experienced professionals to the total volume of business is unusual.

This situation was brought into sharp focus by a talk given by J. Davis Danforth, Executive Vice-President of BBDO and then Chairman of the Board of the American Association of Advertising Agencies. In his talk at the East Central Annual meeting Mr. Danforth reported as follows:

A recent estimate states that there is a total of 50,000-plus people employed in our industry. This is an overall estimate, including clerical help. It might be conservative to say that there are perhaps only 20-25,000 people in the responsible positions in all of the advertising agencies in the United States. That very small number of people is primarily responsible for the creation and placement of billions of dollars of national advertising. In many cases a single client has *more* employees than the total staff of all the advertising agencies in the United States. Actually, 31 members in the Association of National Advertisers employ more than 50 M people each!

This means that, like Alice in Wonderland, these over-busy executives "have to run twice as fast just to stand still" . . . just to keep up with their daily activities for their clients. Keeping ahead of ever-growing competition prevents them from doing the educational job with trainees or beginners, which they would like to do. The best that most executives can do is give a talk before the company training group, or be a one-shot guest speaker at a school or university.

The result of this unfortunate situation is that many advertising courses (outside of night school classes) are taught by professional teachers, who are not *experienced* practitioners of advertising and its related areas. They do a good job of teaching, but cannot give their students the benefit of first-hand, on-the-job advertising experience.

This is no fault of the teaching profession. It's just the mathematical result of too few practitioners, with so many classes to cover.

Despite the excellent teachers' manuals, there is no substitute for the day-to-day experience of working in advertising and its allied fields. So how do we pass on to our new young people the current experiences and accumulated knowledge of our "professionals"? How do we share their successes, failures, findings, and astute observations? One way is to put together a book with each chapter written by an experienced leader in his field of activities.

That is the basic concept of this self-improvement book. Each chapter is written by a "Dean." Many are regular contributors to their trade's publications. Each contributor has put down twenty things he has learned in twenty years. It's as if he or she were talking to the son of some good friend, who was entering our business, and wanted some fatherly advice.

You will discover that the writing style of the contributors varies. This is because no editorial formula was forced on the writers. Therefore they expressed themselves in their own natural way. This we believe provides a change of pace that makes the book more interesting to read.

In some cases the things learned are general. In other cases they are most specific. In all cases the advice comes from out of the wide and deep experience of the writer.

No symposium or business school seminar could hope to secure all these key speakers at one session. Yet they are all here between the covers of this one book.

In most cases the "things learned" are all in the field known so well by the contributor. Yet sometimes the contributors make valuable observations in other areas.

You'll notice that some chapters contain more than twenty points while others have fewer than twenty. This is again because the contributors were not held to a strict editorial formula. They wrote exactly as they wanted . . . about what they wanted . . . as long or short as they wanted. This freedom, we believe, helped assure the extra interest of a compendium by twenty-four authors.

This is not a text book. It begins where most text books leave off. The findings and discoveries of the contributors fill in many of the open spaces of text books. They form a transition from the general to the specific . . . from the theory to the practical situation.

It is hoped that this compendium will be "must reading" for students in advertising public relations, packaging research and the other areas in this broad business of activating the consumer market.

THE EDITOR

How to Write Ads That $ell

23 Ad Executives
Share Their SECRETS for Creating
Advertising That Will Get Attention,
Win Over Customers, and Make Money

Lee Hastings Bristol

Hamilton College awarded Lee Hastings Bristol Ph.D. in 1914 and LL.D. in 1952. He joined Bristol-Myers Company in 1925 as Secretary and Advertising Manager. There he pioneered in radio advertising. Elected Vice President and Director 1928 . . . Executive Vice President 1945 . . . President 1948 . . . Chairman of the Board 1958.

Former Director, Vice-Chairman of Advertising Council; National Chairman, Negro College Fund; Director, NAM; Director, National Conference of Christians and Jews. Author of *Profiles in Advance.*

Eager Beaver and the Voice of Experience

[signature: Lee H. Bristol]

1. EAGER BEAVER: What is your definition of advertising?[1]

    VOICE OF EXPERIENCE: Advertising is the most economical means of informing people of the merits and desirability of a product or service. This embraces all the various media, i.e., newspapers, magazines, radio, T-V, direct mail, car cards, billboards, sky-writing, ad infinitum. The judgment of what is economical is naturally based on following ratios of costs and results.

2. EAGER BEAVER: Why do we have national advertising?

    VOICE OF EXPERIENCE: National advertising exists because there is competition. If there were no choice of products or if the government owned all properties and products, then there would be no need for advertising since choice would be eliminated. Indeed, it isn't strange that one-candidate elections occur in countries where advertising is either nonexistent or relatively unimportant. Where choice exists, you will find a free economy and a free people and national advertising.

3. EAGER BEAVER: How do you gauge your advertising vis-à-vis competition:[1]

    VOICE OF EXPERIENCE: Usually the most enviable position is to be sufficiently well budgeted to permit "out-spending" your competition. If you are "out-spending" your competition, it presupposes that you have already proven the success of the pulling power of your campaign and have established a formula that provides satisfactory results. This matter of "out-spending" your competition may sound like the cart-before-the-horse, but actually, it is good, simple logic in view of the other factors that make "out-spending" possible.

4. EAGER BEAVER: What is one of the first factors of importance in successful promotion?

    VOICE OF EXPERIENCE : I consider that products, especially their performance, constitute the first item of importance. The product has "gotta-be-good." It must deliver as promised. Be sure and test this factor!

5. EAGER BEAVER: Do you place important emphasis on packaging?

    VOICE OF EXPERIENCE: Decidedly I do. The package and container are very important collateral factors. Indeed, we have had experience with products such as Ban, the deodorant, in which I believe the container and its packaging became its most effective selling point. In the matter of packaging, I would say: test! test! test!

6. EAGER BEAVER: How important do you consider *the copy idea* to be in advertising?

    VOICE OF EXPERIENCE: To my mind it is undoubtedly the outstanding, essential factor in successful advertising.

Since everybody recognizes this, there have grown up many forms of research surveys to probe for the best copy idea. These include motivation research, which was unknown until recently. This type of research is employed a number of ways. The one with which I am personally acquainted is the one conducted by Alfred Politz. He and his firm went further than anyone in getting to the bottom of real motivation and its influence on sales. By a clever use of selected samples, by employing an unusual technique in interviews and many other factors, he feels his technique discloses the *real* motives and not merely impressions. People will honestly tell what they *intend,* to do until their subconscious directs the actions that actually contradict their own predictions. For example, if I were being interviewed on the basis of Politz research I might say that next April I am planning to purchase a Buick automobile. To the best of my knowledge that is the truth when I make that response. On the other hand, factors such as the neighborhood where I live, my own personality, age, economic status, conditions of the national economy, etc., may convince the interviewer that when the "chips are down," I probably will end up buying a Ford or some other lower priced car. It's a search for the absolute and not the "relative" truth, as applied to my motivation.

Another and much older example of the success of a new copy idea is Listerine. For the first twenty years or so of its life, Listerine grew as a mouth wash product to the size of a very successful business. Then when Milton Feasley of the Lambert agency invented the word "Halitosis" and presented Listerine as a cure for this new "disease," it was like finding an entirely new market and a new product. The spectacular result of Listerine's growth during the second period proved that in its first phase it had reached a saturation point—only on the basis of its copy claim at that time. By all means, test! test! test!

7. EAGER BEAVER: Do media change from time to time?

VOICE OF EXPERIENCE: Yes, media basically is a very dynamic factor that reflects changing times. In the early days, newspapers were about the only available media. Then magazines came into the national picture; they skimmed the cream and provided immediate national circulation. Then along came the newspaper supplements. They had some of the characteristics of newspapers as to depth of circulation and of magazines as to scope and more leisurely reading. Then along came automobiles and reading habits changed again. I am sure the Sunday driver has distinctly changed some Sunday newspaper reading habits. He certainly has encouraged the growth of the Sunday supplements which, not being topical as are newspapers would permit a longer reading life throughout the week following the Sunday issue.

There can be little doubt that the advent of T-V, even more than radio, taxed the entertainment resources of magazines in their appeal. The result . . . the last few years has seen the demise of a number of previously important national magazines. After all, there are only twenty-four hours in each day for each individual. Therefore, the competition for an individual's free time is increasing— according to the season . . . according to the interest of the individual . . . according to his environment . . . and according to his economic status.

The recent trend for greater contribution to spending income, among larger numbers of the population, has brought some surprising developments. For example, boating is now, from the standpoint of dollars and cents, second only to automobiles in absorbing the consumer leisure spending dollars. Certainly media should be constantly subject to testing. Everything is mutable and dynamic. Nothing in this area is static. Media either goes ahead or it falls back; your company and its products also go ahead or fall back. Change is the order of the day.

8. EAGER BEAVER: How do you determine adequate weight of advertising?

VOICE OF EXPERIENCE: Of course, there are a number of factors that enter into the establishment of a budget, such as the expense ratios of a product or, conversely, the percentage available for promotion. Also we have to reckon with the amount spent by competition. Then there are the results of field tests. All these elements enter in. Again test! test! test!

9. EAGER BEAVER: What part does merchandising play in today's advertising?

VOICE OF EXPERIENCE: It is undoubtedly assuming an increased and even new importance. This is in large measure due to the self-service trend in more and more retail stores. This trend has reached the point where "take-it-off-the-rack-at-Klein's" type of selling dominates the food and variety stores and is growing in drug stores and hardware stores. Self-service increases the importance of merchandising. Why? Because now the purchaser is influenced more by point-of-sale material . . . special deals and offers . . . position of stock in store and displays. It is the job of merchandising to have all these factors in favor of your brand, and to achieve superiority to competitive brands.

One surefire piece of strategy is to make sure that the point-of-sale material is a close, direct tie-in with the basic theme and main appeal in the product's consumer advertising.

Nowadays, with the growth of shopping centers and the variety of products carried in these supermarkets, the housewife can emerge with a full line of cosmetics from the food store. Certain marketing facts are assuming a new importance. Suburbs are growing in population. As automobiles grow more common, shopping centers are luring the customer away from former sales haunts by providing ease of parking. For example, about twelve years ago, 90 per cent of proprietary articles in the drug field were sold through conventional drug outfits, i.e., retail drug stores, drug wholesalers, etc. Today, 70 per cent of many of these items are now sold through food stores, supermarkets, etc.

With this trend, the factor of merchandising in the sense of getting display for your merchandise in these supermarkets is of paramount importance. No longer is there a clerk whose loyalty to your sales appeal could assert itself to the customer in your behalf. No, the pay-off nowadays is on the rack in the supermarket; there is where appeal in behalf of your products must pay off. *The case for advertising prior to the store visit is being put to the acid test.*

10. EAGER BEAVER: How about scientific and technical research? Is this growing in importance?

VOICE OF EXPERIENCE : Yes, I believe it is in all areas—not only with the advertiser, but as a tool for the advertising agency as well. Scientific and technical research is the open door looking constantly to the future—years or months ahead of you. Through research, we make constant improvements in old products. Here also we have the discovery of invention of new products. Here's where stability and future growth really stem from. The best commercial bets are those companies and/ or organizations which are maintaining and expanding their scientific research in both the area of *fundamental* research and the area of *specific* research addressed to *specific* objectives.

11. EAGER BEAVER: How about *marketing* research?

VOICE OF EXPERIENCE: In these dynamic, changing days, research in the marketing area is more important than ever. It can provide much to check the accuracy of your direction, as well as the accuracy of the results. Figures can be misleading, so be sure this matter of marketing research and the interpretation of its findings are entrusted to the minds of professionals and not to the amateurs.

12. EAGER BEAVER: Should one be concerned with trying to *save* advertising dollars?

VOICE OF EXPERIENCE: I interpret your question to mean the withholding of money from advertising. This will soon prove a false economy. Obviously, a person should make every dollar spent in advertising go further—especially he should make it go further than his competitor's dollar. But never, as long as you have a formula that is working, withhold any possible available money that is earmarked for advertising. Remember, advertising is fundamentally a *spending* operation—not a *withholding* one.

13. EAGER BEAVER: Please clear up this question for me: Why do you dislike the expression "spending money for advertising?"

VOICE OF EXPERIENCE: I think it matters whether you give the expression a positive or a negative twist. *Spending* almost implies "operation down-the-drain" whereas in handling an appropriation for advertising *you are really buying sales.* Indeed, any time you are *not* buying sales with your advertising, you are certainly in trouble! I much prefer the positive approach. The verb "spend" to me is far less attractive and more misleading than the verb buy.

14. EAGER BEAVER: What do you consider the most important asset for an advertising agency man?

VOICE OF EXPERIENCE: I guess it's the old truism about having knowledge of the client's problems and objectives. No man in advertising can ever know too much about his market—his products—his competition and all other factors that touch on the foregoing. If that sounds corny, make the most of it! Incidentally, the word "corny" instead of being a word of opprobrium is really complimentary. Things that stand the test of time are really *classics* and the fact that they have been valid for so long is a tribute to the perennial quality of their virtue.

Humility is a gracious trait in anyone. An open, inquiring mind is not merely rare, but it can be your most valuable asset.

15. EAGER BEAVER: Is advertising becoming an exact science?

VOICE OF EXPERIENCE: I doubt if it ever will. In spite of all the systems, reports, and tests, advertising is not yet an exact science. Practically all final decisions are made by human judgment and are just as fallible as human judgment always is.

16. Now for some points of advice to a younger advertising manager or his understudy.

Cooperate with your agency, but don't just "yes" them. On the other hand, don't heckle. It's petty and unattractive, and it never produces results when overdone. Remember, most agency men know lots more than you do in their field. They generally have far greater and broader experience than you on die other side of the desk.

17. To an agency cub:

There's a big reward for the agency guy who builds up dignity and respect for his agency. Mutual trust between agent and client will certainly bring out the best there is on both sides. To good agency men it isn't unfair heckling to ask, in matters where questions arise, for as much proof or evidence as possible.

18. Remember your advertising reflects you—your company—its principals (as well as principles). Don't let any of them down* This includes your character, your performance, your conduct t all times. Don't get tense; relax! Laughter is the greatest stimulant in the world. Dare to be different or advanced. I will give you an example from my own experience.

In 1925 I was visited by a salesman for NBC who was selling time for Station WEAF. He was trying to sell the use of their station-advertising time for selling our Ipana Toothpaste which was beginning to grow on a national basis. I met resistance on all sides—within our company and within our agency too. Advertising a toothpaste over radio! Nonsense! It's preposterous! It's undignified! People will resent it!

I took on three stations however—one in Boston, one in New York and one in Philadelphia. We put on Sam Lanin, an orchestra leader fairly well-known at the time. The orchestra assembled for the purpose was a good one. The selections were never too highbrow, but were tuneful and melodic with a few semi-classical numbers interpolated. Phil Carlin and Graham McNamee were the announcers and they introduced a little M.C. talk before each number and played much the role of a present-day disc jockey.

I can say unqualifiedly that the whole idea worked out splendidly. We got a new surge of sales that could only be attributed to the new medium—radio. Within a year, we were on a national network and have been so almost continuously since—certainly until the advent of television.

19. Be sure to keep your principal executives—both at the advertiser end of the picture and in the agencies—as much in the know as possible. To negligent communications can too often be attributed misunderstandings and all kinds of other problems.

Two lessons I have learned over the years. The first is about courage and boldness in a depression. The drug business didn't start to fall off as other businesses did right after the stock market crash in 1929. Instead, it had a belated reaction. It wasn't until 1934 that the proprietary drug business felt the full impact of the depression. All proprietary manufacturers then drew in their horns and immediately started cutting appropriations.

I tried an experiment at that time which paid off handsomely. Instead of cutting, I increased our appropriations at that time. I knew I was making an investment in red ink on a short-term basis. However, the tide turned rather quickly and when all of us emerged from that depression, our company had achieved a big head-start over our competition (as contrasted with the competitive standing previously).

MORAL: Don't always follow the crowd.

20. The second lesson over a period of time was brought home to me as a manufacturer.

Don't be afraid to compete against your own products. The newer products you introduce do not entirely steal business from your earlier, established brands. Instead, the two together carve out a bigger piece of the market than would be the case if only one brand were promoted. The big soap companies are conspicuous examples of the efficacy of this policy.

Thomas D'Arcy Brophy

B.A. and Honorary LL.D. degrees at Gonzaga University, B.S. at MIT. Joined Ken-yon & Eckhardt, Inc. in 1931, Vice President in 1934, President in 1944, Chairman of Board from 1952 until his 1958 retirement.

He served as PR Chairman of U.S.O.; Chairman, of the AAAA Board; President of NOAB; recipient of Honorary CBE from British Government; and one of the first AFA awards for public service; Founder and first President of the American Heritage Foundation.

The Role of Advertising in Our Economy

1. We in America live and prosper in a dynamic economy. Ours has been and is an economy of relative abundance which has succeeded in bringing about a material well-being never before known in history. It is an economy which emphasizes consumption! In this country consumption does not necessarily mean wearing out goods in a physical sense. We wear out goods psychologically as well. Our hats are discarded because they are psychologically worn out, not because they are physically done in. Usually our clothes are psychologically worn out and discarded while the material is still good. We dispose of our automobiles when they become obsolete rather than when they are physically worn out. How different is this viewpoint from the practices that are current in other nations—England and France, for instance!

It is difficult for the European to understand the economic importance of the individual in our country and the

American idea of psychological obsolescence. It is also incomprehensible to most that in America we spend nearly eight billion dollars a year for advertising!

Why do we do it? What is advertising's role in our economy? What useful purpose does advertising serve?

I shall undertake to develop my observations why advertising is essential to our dynamic way of life:

> First,   *advertising makes jobs.*
>
> Second,   *advertising reduces selling costs.*
>
> Third,   *advertising increases company -profits.*
>
> Fourth,   *advertising increases company security.*
>
> and finally,   *our enormous and growing productivity needs advertising to speed up consumption.*

2. Advertising makes more jobs for more people. Yes, it is a fact that by creating a growing demand for new products, advertising makes jobs. A few examples. The automobile, of course, is the classic one. To be sure, it eliminated the village smithy, the buggy maker, and the livery stable, but it revolutionized our way of living and it opened opportunities never before possible. When you think what has been accomplished in the era of the automobile—when you think of all the jobs that are made possible by the five million and more automobiles sold in the United States every year, when you think what this has meant in the way of new jobs, ranging all the way from the thousands of motels, restaurants and gas stations, to the enormous development of our national parks, it gives some idea of what the automobile has con-tributed to our society.

Was it the first automobile, or the first hundred, or the first thousand that brought this about? No! It was the mass production of customers for automobiles that has brought the automobile to its present importance in our economy. Mass consumption made mass production possible and advertising is largely responsible for bringing about mass consumption—and the jobs—that the development of the automobile has created.

To cite another example in a totally different field—deodorants. Remember the day not so long ago when Lifebuoy was the only deodorant product with any appreciable volume? Today the deodorant business has grown to major proportions, and this has been accomplished without taking away from any other business, including perfumes! This is another example where demand created by mass consumption methods resulted in a new industry with attendant jobs, and one which has been developed without taking away from any existing business.

The new instant dessert puddings can be cited as another example. Puddings have not moved as rapidly as they might have in recent years. Along came the instant pudding and look what happened. Sales of all dessert puddings are up one-third as the result of the introduction of something new, the instant pudding, which revitalized an old and somewhat static business by the introduction of a new product idea, extensively promoted through advertising.

It all adds up to the fact that mass consumption makes mass production possible and mass production means more jobs. Advertising, because of its ability to accelerate the regular acceptance of new products and to lift the level of acceptability of established products, unleashes a tremendous flood of new demand—and new employment.

The critics say advertising causes people to spend needlessly. By a narrow definition this may be true. But our whole economy, which has brought us so much prosperity, emphasizes consumption. And psychological obsolescence is a factor of importance in that consumption.

What advertising does, and does well, is to increase what might be called the "wantability" of goods. The more wantable goods become, the greater the prospect that money will be exchanged for those goods and this in turn spells continued employment and more jobs.

3. Advertising increases marketing efficiency, reduces costs, and increases our standard of living. In discussing this I am not going back into the past. Instead I shall consider only the present and the future and I'll take supermarket merchandising as an example. We in advertising are acutely aware of what has happened in the marketing and merchandising of grocery and drug products in the last few years. But I wonder if the growth of self-service is fully realized. According to Neilsen surveys in 1956, 63.3% of all grocery sales were through self-service outlets! Now what is the secret of the supermarkets? Is it availability? Abundance? Convenience? Possibly, but those advantages would never have worked without something else. What has made supermarkets successful has been primarily the fact that customers are pre-sold to a greater extent than ever before. They go in to buy. This has resulted in unprecedented traffic through supermarkets and a much faster turnover of goods. The success of the supermarket has been due primarily to the speed-up of store traffic and increased marketing efficiency related directly to the fast movement of goods. This largely is the result of the sales effectiveness of advertising.

4. I would like to say a few words about the sales effectiveness of advertising. There has been a tendency in recent years to discount the ability of advertising to sell. It has been said that advertising paves the way, that it facilitates selling; that it does this, that and the other thing, but there is a tendency to deprecate advertising

as a seller of goods. One of the dangers I see today that should concern all of us in this field is the misuse of advertising, or perhaps it should be called the disuse of advertising, in its primary and fundamental function of selling goods and services. It is not enough to use advertising simply to promote premium offers, consumer deals and the bringing about of better store displays. If the role of advertising in selling is limited to that, it is a poor role indeed. Advertising should sell goods, and good advertising does it!

Such advertising is responsible for the pre-sold customer, which has made supermarket merchandising and the self-service store so successful. Insofar as advertising fails in its primary function of selling goods and services, we may have serious doubts as to its efficiency. So let's not over-emphasize the fringe uses of advertising. I do not mean to imply, of course, that advertising should never be used to promote deals, premiums, etc. Of course it should, but we should never forget that the primary purpose of advertising is to sell goods and services and we in advertising had better realize it if we are to live up to our own billing that advertising is the most important factor in the manufacturing of mass consumption. Advertising must sell. It must sell goods. It must sell services. It cannot avoid that responsibility.

5. From the manufacturer's viewpoint, the problems in today's economy are, first, the gaining of customers and, second, the holding of them. As the personal salesman becomes less and less important in many fields, these problems become major concerns. To give you an idea of the importance of gaining customers, there are 4,000,000 births in the country every year. What an opportunity that presents to the manufacturers of all products for infants! It also presents a problem—a changing market every year.

Statisticians tell us that a 25 per cent average increase in marriages will take place by 1959-1960, due primarily to the war babies coming of age. Consider what 25 per cent average increase in marriages will mean. New families to be cultivated. Millions of people entering into a new era of wanting many goods. We have to sell 2,000,000 new family units per year. Not for one year, but for many years.

On the other hand, 600,000 people die each year between the ages of 25 and *65* and almost as many go out of markets for other reasons. So the problem of the manufacturer is not only one of gaining new customers, and compensating for the loss of old, but the constant need to recruit new customers from the 48,000,000 households already in existence in the United States.

6. Market Research Corporation studies disclose that there is little comfort in the idea of a permanent customer. Such an individual is a relatively infrequent occurrence. Professor George Brown of the University of Chicago, in analyzing the results of the *Chicago Tribune* data on customer loyalty, reported the following facts:

    17 per cent of the families are loyal to one brand of soup. The rest have little, if any, loyalty to any brand.

    13 per cent of the families are loyal to one brand of cereal. The rest have little, if any, loyalty to any one brand.

    27 per cent of the families are loyal to one brand of concentrated orange juice. The rest have little, if any, brand loyalty.

    47 per cent of the families are loyal to one brand of coffee— and in coffee you would think loyalty would be extremely high because of taste condition. It just doesn't seem to be so.

7. Similarly, in studies conducted by our own research department, we have found repeatedly that it takes two

or three experimental or first-time buyers to produce one frequent or regular customer. Because of factors like these, the problem of maintaining and increasing customer patronage is a constant, unrelenting one. Our job in advertising is to increase the efficiency of marketing and selling by addressing ourselves to a number of interrelated responsibilities—the cultivation of new customers as they come into the buying age, the cultivation and re-cultivation of established families—to help maintain their present patronage.

Supermarket or self-service marketing does not mean automatic merchandising. It is not enough just to have distribution. The supermarket merchandiser wants, and rightfully expects the pre-selling of goods and must have pre-selling to speed store traffic, increase turnover, conserve shelf space, and reduce waste. Only in these ways is marketing efficiency achieved and only through advertising can these things be accomplished.

8. Advertising tends to increase company profits by increasing company sales at the lowest cost for doing so. It seems to me I have heard it said that advertising increases the cost of goods, so it is important to get the record straight. The cost of selling covers personal selling, promotion and advertising. All are necessary to the job of producing customers and developing customer good will. But the least expensive, if it is employed effectively, is advertising.

9. Some consumers have a strange idea about the cost of advertising. I am not going to belabor the point because you have heard the arguments. You know that the cost of advertising a well-known brand of soup is only one-sixth of a cent per can. You know too that in the case of a nationally known breakfast food, the cost of advertising is only three-tenths of a cent per 15-cent package. And the cost of advertising an automobile is just about the added cost of white-walled tires! In Cincinnati recently I

heard some thing interesting about Ivory Soap. Seventy-five years ago a 6- ounce cake of Ivory sold for a nickel. The same 6-ounce cake of Ivory Soap, a much better product actually, can be bought today three cakes for a quarter. Think of it! For seventy-five years the price of Ivory Soap has remained almost constant, despite all the cost increases that have taken place, not only in recent years, but over that long, long period! In seventy-five years the cost of raw materials, the cost of labor, the cost of everything has gone up. The one thing that has made it possible to keep the cost of Ivory Soap substantially where it was seventy-five years ago is mass consumer demand, developed and sustained by advertising.

It has been the mass production of customers which has made possible the economies and efficiency of mass production. So, the ideas of some consumers about the cost of advertising are far off the beam, and there is need for those of us in advertising to know the facts and give voice to them whenever a suitable opportunity is presented.

Management too sometimes has peculiar ideas about the cost of advertising, and those of us who deal with management must be prepared to answer some searching questions. Let's not forget that executives, long occupied with the problems of production, labor and finance, are sometimes not as well informed about the cost of distribution as they are about the things with which they had been preoccupied during the long period of seller's market. But in the transition from a seller's to a buyer's market, the success of a business shifts from capacity to produce to ability to sell, and in many businesses volume and profit will depend on the mass production of customers at the lowest possible cost. So these executives should know more about advertising and its costs than they have in the past, and it is up to us to inform them. Of course, the attitude of top management toward advertising and, for that matter, its interest in advertising, naturally will vary with different types of business. The cigarette manufacturer looks upon advertising in quite a different light than the manufacturer of building materials, but it may be said generally that top management is not as aware of advertising, how it should be used, and what it can do, as it should be.

10. Some time ago, Dun & Bradstreet studied the performance of individual enterprises in thirty-two types of industries and found that those businesses which had a high ratio of advertising to sales expense were more profitable than those which had a lower ratio of advertising to sales expense. The former had a ratio of advertising to total selling expense over the latter by a margin of 36 per cent. Other factors may have been operative, but over and above these other factors is the persistent trend of a higher investment in advertising for the profitable companies than for the unprofitable ones.

In case you think I am placing too much emphasis on advertising in selling, may I hasten to say that efficient production through product research, good labor relations, and sound fiscal policies, all these elements of business, are of great importance, but I submit that in the opinion of too many, distribution and its basic problem today of mass-producing customers has been overshadowed by preoccupation with mass-producing goods.

11. matter of fact, it is a good thing to remember that the production problem in any business is only over when the goods are in the hands of the ultimate customer, or to phrase it another way, today manufacturers must not only produce the goods, they must also produce the customers—in order to produce a profit! The primary purpose of advertising is to produce the customer, and if advertising is to be accorded a place in proportion to its economic importance in this light, it is essential that it be recognized, not as a competitor to profits, but as an ingredient of profits.

12. rtising increases company security. By that, I mean it increases the chances for individual businesses to survive, which is important both to owners and employees.

Only a consumer franchise provides security for many businesses. Recently one of the best-known investment services, in commemorating its thirty-fifth anniversary, listed the twenty most favored stocks in 1919. General Motors, RCA, and several others of today's "blue chips" were not included. Listed were several which are no longer important in American business, and only a few would be included on a list of today's most favored stocks. Thirty-five years is not a long time, but it could represent the life cycle of a business, unless that business keeps abreast of the times and continues to have a solid consumer franchise.

That advertising contributes to this type of company security is well illustrated by the history of a food manufacturer, the first in its field today, as it was thirty-five years ago. This company has survived three changes in management but it is still tops because its brands are household names in America, the result of constant and effective advertising.

13. The mass production of customers is the only avenue to stability and security for the individual   company in our dynamic economy—and this applies with equal force to retailer and to manufacturer.

14. Advertising is not expendable. It is not a garnishment of business. It is an essential ingredient of our economy. It is to selling what the machine is to production. Advertising mass-produces customers for a mass-production economy. It makes jobs. It reduces selling costs. It helps increase our standard of living. Effectively and properly used, it increases company profits and it makes possible the only security a company can hope to have in an uncertain world. Advertising is indeed the Cinderella of American business.

15. Advertising today faces different challenges than advertising did last year, five years ago, ten years ago. Cinderella must be as modern as the times if she is to keep her place in the business picture.

16. Today, more than ever before in our generation, the chips are down. Our tremendous productive economy is capable of producing goods and services at a rate never before achieved. On the train last evening I read some interesting statistics. In December of 1956 expenditures for plant and equipment in this country were 19 per cent greater than in December of 1955. Electric power production was five per cent greater. Personal income was up 6.1 per cent. Production is on the march! But unless it is possible to increase the wantability of products this total potential productive capacity will not be fully used. And if it is not fully used, it will mean the existence of idle resources. And idle resources mean idle people.

17. To meet this growing challenge, the selling of goods and services via advertising requires that we know more and more about the consumer, his or her buying habits, her motivations, her likes and prejudices. The answer is research. We must know more about the intimate process of consumer decision-making and consumer buying actions.

18. Here the new breed of researcher who is a specialist in the field of communication of ideas and in the study of factors related to consumer buying will play a vital role in increasing the consumer responsiveness to advertising. Active interplay between such research specialists and top-notch advertising men is bound to increase the effectiveness of the advertising. The results of such contributions in the past few years are plainly evident

in terms of any measurement of advertising we care to make—from post testing of individual advertisements for their effectiveness to actual success stories in terms of sales response.

19. Even though we have made great progress in this area, the future literally bristles with promise as we team up the advertising man and the researcher. Our ability to get to the taproots of consumer motivation, our ability to increase people's emotional and rational response to advertising will increase progressively as our studies continually develop methods for communicating to the essential areas of consumer response. This does not mean that the basic "building blocks" of human response to advertising will be completely laid out in a formula for all time. What it means instead is that we are arriving at a near scientific and orderly process in exploring the areas in which advertising can produce most effectively. And because people do change as conditions change, we can rest assured that no problem will be permanently solved.

This rational exploration into the real dynamics of consumer demand will permit advertising to rise to full maturity as a tool of business. It will be a time during which the intuitive ad man and the one who plays the hunches alone will have to give way to the teaming up of creative thinking and research.

20. The same general integration between merchandising, promotion, and research is similarly emerging. This is helping advertisers to set up promotional activities which are completely relevant to the problems which a particular product or service has. It is helping advertisers to set more realistic goals for promotions, and to make use of them when there is an important marketing objective to be reached. It is helping to understand more fully the basic value of premiums, promotions, special offers,

etc.; it tells who takes advantage of them and what effect it has upon building brand images and building brand patronage.

This then is the pattern of the new advertising to meet the challenge of the marketing future. These group activities will furthermore be given broad overall direction and guidance through the development of a basic marketing plan. Prepared by competent marketing people who understand the circumstances in which the advertiser's brand is competing, and aided and abetted by market facts, such a marketing plan is in reality the counterpart of the blueprint in architecture. Before money is spent on advertising in the future, the marketing plan must set forth and document in detail the marketing objectives, the brand resources which are available, the competitive environment in the industry, and the promotional goals which must be set up if the basic marketing plan is to work.

This, I believe, is the kind of thinking and action which is called for if American advertising is to meet the challenge of keeping consumption abreast of ever-increasing production, so that all in America may continue to enjoy the fruits of the dynamic economy which is the basis of our American way of life.

John Caples

Vice president of Batten, Barton, Durstine & Osborn, Inc. Born New York City. Horace Mann School. Graduated U. S. Naval Academy (Annapolis). Started a famous advertising technique with ads headlined "They laughed when I sat down at the piano," and 'They grinned when the waiter spoke to me in French." Taught courses in advertising at Columbia. Lecturer at advertising clubs and conventions. Commander, U. S. Navy in World War II. Author of four textbooks on advertising including *Tested Advertising Methods* and *Making Ads Pay.*

21 Things I've Learned in 20 Years

John Caples

AUTHOR'S NOTE: The reason I have included 21 things instead of 20 things is because last year 1 learned two things. It was an especially good year!

1. THE MOST IMPORTANT PART OF AN AD IS THE HEADLINE.

If you can think up a good headline which selects the right audience and offers them a benefit, you can almost certainly produce a good ad. Your copy can simply be a continuation of the idea you expressed in your headline.

On the other hand, if your ad has a poor headline, you almost certainly have a poor ad, because people will not read the copy.

You may say—How about the basic selling appeal? Isn't that important? The answer is, yes, it is important and the *headline usually contains the basic selling appeal.* For example, the headline "How I retired on a guaranteed income for life" contains the basic selling appeal of financial security after retirement.

You may say—How about the illustration used in an ad? Isn't that important? The answer is yes. However, *the illustration is usually determined by the headline.* For example, the retirement income ads used by the Phoenix Mutual Life Insurance Company are illustrated with pictures of happily retired people.

Therefore, in writing an ad, you should give a great deal of attention to headline writing. Write a lot of headlines and then put them aside for a while. Then go back and select the best headline.

2. YOU SHOULD PROMISE BENEFITS.

What is the most important element in a headline? It is usually the *'promise of benefits.* You can use a direct promise or an implied promise. Here is a headline which contains a direct promise.

New shampoo leaves your hair smoother—easier to manage. Here is a headline which contains an implied promise:

Imagine me . . . holding an audience spellbound for 30 minutes

The reader figures that by reading the copy in this ad, he too may learn the secret of holding an audience spellbound.

Here are other examples of headlines that contain promises.

The secret of making people like you I lost my bulges and saved money too Who else wants a lighter cake—in half the mixing time?

3. CURIOSITY IS A POWERFUL TOOL.

One method for writing a successful headline is to include two elements as follows: (1) a promise of benefits, and (2) a curiosity-arousing element. Example:

How a "fool stunt" made me a star salesman

This headline arouses curiosity with the words "fool stunt." And it promises a benefit with the words "star salesman."

Here are other examples:

How a strange accident saved me from baldness

How a new discovery made a plain girl beautiful How I made a fortune with a "crazy idea"

4. YOU MUST MAKE YOUR MEANING CLEAR.

Make your meaning clear if you want to make a sale. For example, notice the clearness of the following mail order headlines:

Reduce as you walk . . . wonder girdle takes 4 inches off

Stop cat and dog damage . . . $1.00

Free . . . Home and garden ideas you can use

These mail order ads have to produce sales at a profit or else the advertiser will go out of business.

For the sake of contrast, read the following unclear headlines from general ads whose sales results are not traceable.

Stays time in its flight

Space travel

Directing diversified interests

Moral: If you want a lesson in printed salesmanship, read some mail order ads. Read especially the mail order ads which you see repeated again and again. Those are the ads that are paying off in sales.

5. PEOPLE LIKE TO READ LISTS OF RULES.

People like to read numbered lists of rules and methods.

For example, here are some chapter headings from one of the best selling books of modern times, *How to Win Friends and Influence People.*

1. Six ways to make people like you
2. Twelve ways to win people to your way of thinking

3. Nine ways to change people without giving offense or arousing resentment

4. Seven rules for making your home life happier

Another example comes from the best-selling book of all time, namely, that famous list of rules known as "The Ten Commandments."

6. HOW TO APPEAL TO BOTH MEN AND WOMEN.

Sometimes you can increase the readership of your ad if you can write a headline which arouses the interest of *both men and women.* For example, here is the title of a *Reader's Digest* article which does this:

Why husbands don't talk to their wives

Men will read this article to find out why other men keep silent in the presence of their wives. And women will read it to find out why their husbands aren't talking.

Here are three more headings which appeal to both men and women:

How to live with a woman

What's wrong with American men?

Advice to wives whose husbands don't save money

7. YOU CAN OVERCOME BAD NEWS WITH GOOD NEWS.

One aid to selling is to admit in the headline of your ad that the proposition you are selling is going to cost the reader something. You might object to this on the grounds that this is telling the bad news too soon and that the bad news or price tag should appear at the end of the ad. However, you can overcome this by putting good news into the headline as well as bad news. For example:

Is $40 a day worth 4¢ stamp?

This headline tells the reader that you are going to require him to use a 4¢ stamp to find out about your proposition. This is bad news. However, the good news ($40 a day) is such very good news that the 4$ stamp seems small by comparison. Here are two other headlines that use this technique.

How $7 started me on the road to $12,000 a year

How I turned $1000 into a million in real estate—in my
    spare time

8. THE MOKE YOU TELL, THE MORE YOU SELL.

A lesson you can learn from mail order advertisers is the sales value of including in an ad a telegraphic presentation of *many benefits.* For example, here is copy from one of the mail order ads mentioned above:

Stop cat and dog damage . . . $1.00

Dog wicks are the perfect solution for repelling pets. One sniff and away they'll run. Hang this chemical wick on shrub or branch and rest easy for the whole season. Safe, harmless to animals. Use inside or out—protects lawns, garbage pails, flowers, furniture. Trains your pets and neighbors' dogs. Guaranteed to do the job or your money back. Pack of 20 for $1, postage paid.

9. SPECIFIC COPY IS MORE BELIEVABLE.

The headline, "How I Made $20 Last Week," is not as believable as "How I Saved $19.83 Last Week."

An example of specific copy is the famous Ivory Soap slogan "99 44/100 pure."

Here are some other examples of copy that is believable because it is specific:

Take any 3 of these Kitchen appliances—for only $8.95 (Values up to $15.45)

Pierced by 301 Nails . . . retains full air pressure (automobile tires)

161 new ways to a man's heart—in this fascinating book for cooks

10. SELECT YOUR AUDIENCE.

Here are the headlines of two ads that were tested against each other by means of a split-run copy test:

1.   Car owners—save one gallon of gas in every ten

2.   Save one gallon of gas in every ten

Each ad contained the same hidden offer in which people were invited to write for a sample of the product. Ad number one, beginning with the words "Car owners," pulled 27% more sample requests.

11. USE TESTIMONIALS.

You can increase the selling power of your copy by including one or more testimonials from satisfied users. Mail order advertisers do this all the time.

12. A FORMULA FOR WRITING GOOD COPY.

If you want a good ad, you should write a lot of copy and then boil it down.

For example, if you want 500 words of copy you should begin by writing 1500 words. Then go over it and cut out all the nonessentials. Omit unnecessary sentences and weak phrases. Make it telegraphic, fast moving and fact packed. A piece of copy is like a pot of broth—the more you boil it down, the stronger the flavor gets.

13. REPEAT IMPORTANT POINTS.

If you want to make a dent in a prospect's mind, you should repeat important points. For example, you can increase the pulling power of an ad by saying in the headline, "Free offer." Then in the first part of the copy you can say, "This offer costs you nothing." And at the end of the ad you can say, "Send no money" or "Don't pay a penny."

14. HOW TO FIND OUT WHAT PEOPLE THINK OF AN AD.

Don't show somebody an ad and say, "Here is an ad I just wrote; what do you think of it?" The chances are that the other person will try to please you by saying, "I think it's fine."

You can get a more accurate judgment of your efforts by show-ing a person *two* ads and saying, "Here are two ads. Which do you like better?"

After your respondent has selected an ad you may be able to get further help by saying, "Why do you like that ad better?"

15. PUT YOUR AD WHERE IT WILL BE SEEN.

The two most important things in advertising are:

1. **What you say in advertisements**

2. **Where you say it**

What you say involves copy. Where you say it involves media. Proper use of media means putting your message where it will get into the minds of the largest number of prospects at the lowest cost.

For example, one of the surest ways to help an ad pull coupons or get a high readership rating is to beg, borrow or steal the first right hand page position in the magazine in which you are running your ad.

16. SIZE OF CIRCULATION IS NOT THE ONLY MEASUREMENT OF MEDIA VALUE.

In considering the advertising value of a publication you should not only consider the price per page per 1000 circulation but also how the circulation is obtained. To cite an extreme case, a subscription to a publication which is obtained by giving away a free dictionary is not likely to be as valuable as a subscription that is obtained on the merits of the publication alone.

17. CLAIMS MADE BY MEDIA MUST BE WEIGHED AGAINST EACH OTHER.

Almost all media salesmen can point to a survey or to a set of statistics that makes that particular newspaper or magazine or network sound "best" in some respects such as:

"Largest circulation in the financial field" "fastest growing broadcasting station in the West" "lowest cost per reader among sporting goods buyers" "highest income per reader in this area"

These claims are usually true. However, it takes skill to interpret the various claims in respect to your special needs.

Hint: You can get plenty of help in finding any flaws in a survey made by one publication if you will talk with the representative of a competitive publication.

18. MEDIA SALESMEN CAN HELP YOU.

It is good to hear the sales talks for various media direct from the media salesmen who call on you. You can pick up valuable bits of information about trends in advertising from media men.

Also, by seeing them personally, you can retain the good will of this important group of emissaries who are constantly meeting your clients and your prospects. Ben Duffy, Vice Chairman of the Board of BBDO, said: "You should not be too busy to see media salesmen. These men know that you cannot always buy their wares. But they do appreciate the opportunity to tell their stories."

19. TAKE THE EASY SALES FIRST.

It is good to understand the method of skimming the cream from a market. This is the method employed by mail order advertisers when they advertise for the easy-to-get customers in certain media. When the cost per sale gets too high in the original media, the wise mail order advertiser switches to other media or to other areas so that he can pick up some additional easy-to-get customers. This system of shifting media is like fishing. The experienced fisherman shifts from one location to another in order to catch more fish.

20. KEEP PENCIL AND PAPER WITH YOU ALWAYS.

Ideas usually come slowly when you sit down at your desk and say to yourself, "Now I'm going to think up some ideas." Your mind is apt to become a blank and the pad in front of you is likely to remain blank.

Many of your best ideas come to you in fleeting moments such as:

When you are riding in a bus When you wake up in the morning When you are shaving When you are walking along the street When you are talking with someone When you are reading a newspaper When you are going to sleep at night

Therefore keep pencil and pad with you at all times, even by your bedside. Write your ideas down the minute you think of them. Otherwise many of your best ideas may be lost forever.

21. BE ENTHUSIASTIC.

If you want to sell an idea to another person, do it when you are enthusiastic about it. Don't wait until the idea has cooled off in your mind because then some uncertainty and doubt may creep into your voice. The great philosopher Goethe said to a visitor, "Tell me the things you are sure of. I have doubts enough of my own."

Bennett S. Chapple, Jr.

After graduating from Antioch College, 1927, Bennett Chappie went with American Rolling Mill Co. He joined Carnegie-Illinois Steel Corporation as Manager of Sales Promotion. Subsequently served as Vice President in charge of emergency defense coordination. Made Assistant to President, Firth Sterling Steel Co., 1944. Went with United States Steel Corporation 1947, as Vice President in charge of Sales. Elected Assistant Executive Vice President of Sales. Now is Administrative Vice President, Commercial. Served as President of the National Industrial Advertising Association, 1950-51.

25 Things I've Learned in 20 Years

Bennett S Chapple Jr.

1. Try constantly to wring the last nickel's worth out or an individual ad in the way of merchandising and promotion. In many cases these side benefits will justify the advertising before it has even appeared.

2. In merchandising advertising use "preprints," not "reprints," whenever possible. Advance information flatters as well as in forms the recipient.

3. Before preparing any advertising program, put down the specific things you want that advertising to accomplish. Don't be general and make sure the objectives are attainable and the results at least partially measurable. Sell your program to management on the basis of these objectives and then proceed to measure your progress toward the objectives on a planned basis.

4. One of the biggest problems of advertising management is to encourage creative thinking but keep it channeled in the proper direction. It helps when you keep creative

people—writers, artists, photographers, etc.—fully informed on objectives, progress, comments, etc. When an idea is rejected, tell them why.

5. Although readership scores and other measurements of the effectiveness of individual ads may not be exact, they do provide some sort of bench mark in a campaign. Feed such information to all people who have a hand in the campaign—bad ratings as well as good.

6. Keep in mind that the basic purpose of all advertising is communication. When you increase readership, viewing, listening or what have you ten per cent in any campaign, you have in effect added hundreds, thousands or even millions of dollars in real advertising value to your efforts.

7. Most advertising executives use motion pictures as a part of a promotional program. In planning a film, make sure two important points are agreed upon before creative talent goes to work. (1) What are the objectives of the film? (2) Exactly what and who will be the audience for the film and how will you reach that audience? Making a film before such decisions are made is like producing an ad and then deciding whether to run it in the *Ladies Home Journal* or *Engineering News-Record.*

8. Environment for advertising is a subject that sometimes be comes buried in the avalanche of circulation, readership and audience numbers. The best advertising takes advantage of the mood of the reader, viewer or listener which is somewhat dependent on the environment created by the newspaper, magazine, or TV or radio show.

9. In media selection, "Don't try to fill the wheelbarrow with a teaspoon but don't use a steam-shovel, either." Try to pick the media that will reach the people you want, but

watch out! Don't buy too many or too few. In the first case you're likely to be wasting a lot of money; in the second, you're likely to fall short of your objective.

10. Don't underestimate the helpfulness of a good media representative. He can help keep you posted not only on his medium, but also on market conditions, competitive activity, distributor or retailer reaction.

11. In thinking about your own organization, try to draw the line between the functions that are responsible for the "big ideas" (campaigns, overall approaches, copy platforms, etc.) and those whose job it is to produce the "smaller ideas" (headlines, copy, individual art treatment, etc.) Some people are good in the first area and poor in the second, and vice-versa. In administering advertising one of the big jobs is to keep the smaller ideas from running away with the bigger ones.

12. In preparing a new program, don't overlook the chance of increasing impact and effectiveness through a joint effort with another advertiser or group. (Drapes, rugs and furniture go with wallpaper; electric utilities with electric appliances; sheets with mattresses; syrup with pancakes, etc.). Don't overdo this, however, or you're likely to lose your identity.

13. In business and trade papers, don't overlook the use of inserts. You pay for the printing, it's true, but you have the advantage of special stock, colors and layout usually at black and white rates. Reprints generally make good mailing pieces.

14. In introducing a new product or a product improvement, don't forget the possibilities of product publicity. Schedule your advertising so you don't "pull the cork" on publicity being released.

15. Never "oversell" the effects of an individual ad or a complete program. Promise only what you are sure you can deliver. Anything extra will be a feather in your cap.

16. Attend advertising club and association meetings. One good idea from such contacts wall pay for the time and money expended.

17. Accept speaking assignments on advertising and let people know you are available for speeches. You will not only benefit by the wider acquaintanceship developed by such contacts but preparing a speech will consolidate your thinking and stimulate ideas.

18. Have solitary "brainstorm" sessions. When facing a problem or seeking an idea, get a big pad of paper in front of you, a pencil in your hand and start thinking. Write down everything you can think of about the subject, no matter how wild the thoughts are. Keep it up and you will find your ideas channeling into practical patterns. The "Big Idea" may come sooner than you think. If it doesn't work, put it away for a while and start again. Believe me, it often works.

19. No matter what advertising function you perform, become an advertising expert. Learn all you can about printing methods, type, layout, engraving, media, production, etc. It will be rewarding and you never know when it will cause a knock from opportunity.

20. If you have an idea to sell to the boss, don't pop it out in a burst of enthusiasm. Remember the count-down is important to a successful launching. Think it through. Anticipate the questions and objections. Be prepared to defend it. Use imagination in your presentation. If it is good, it will sell itself, providing you give it the proper ground support.

21. Be a self-starter. If you're a true advertising man you're an idea man. Don't wait for assignments. Create activities that you working Saturdays and Sundays. If you don't enjoy your work enough to do this, get out of the advertising business.

22. Set your sights on the man ahead of you and get his job. Get it by getting to know as much as he knows and get it by helping him do his work so much better that you push him up to the job ahead of him.

23. Train the people under you so they can do your job. If you're as good as you should be, you have nothing to worry about. They won't get your job until you're ready to move up and you won't be overlooked for that promotion just because there is no one to replace you.

24. Know all there is to know about your company and its products. Next to the president no one should know more than the advertising man. You are the company's spokesman. How can you speak well if you don't know?

25. If you are in a position to select an assistant, choose him with greater care than you would a wife. Many are the successes of advertising men that can be traced to the effective support of a good assistant. He must be energetic, ambitious, honest, loyal, and, above all, creative, but beyond all these he must be the man who can take your place.

Edwin W. Ebel

E dwin W. Ebel, Vice President in charge of Advertising for General Foods Corporation, joined General Foods in 1948 after having served in executive capacities with leading advertising agencies. Mr. Ebel is a member of the board of directors of The Advertising Council, the Advertising Federation of America, and the American Institute of Food Distribution. He is a former chairman of the board of the Association of National Advertisers and a founder member of the American Marketing Society.

Expose Yourself to People

Ed Ebel

***If you like people, advertising can be a
very satisfying career.***

1. One of the prime satisfactions is that as long as you
   are in advertising, you have to "stay with it." That
   is not merely because techniques of advertising
   continually change—techniques change in all dynamic
   businesses. It is chiefly because people's interests
   constantly change. And this is most important because
   it is largely through people's interest in the world about
   them that we are able to get a selling message into their
   consciousness.

2. The advertising business is for men or women who
   like to work hard. It is not a nine-to-five business.
   It is not just a business of research and planning,
   of layouts and copy, of schedules and finished
   art, of media and discounts and closing dates, of
   reach and frequency and circulation. These are merely
   the tools of advertising. The most important thing in
   advertising is getting to know people and what makes
   people tick and how to influence them.

3. The more you know about people, the better an advertising man you will make. The fact is that advertising comes easiest to the man who is naturally interested in people, who has an insatiable interest in people and in how to reach and influence them.

A person going into advertising should make efforts to develop himself not merely by reading advertising textbooks, but by having a hearty appetite for books about people. An interest in psychology and sociology is a decided advantage.

I think there are several stages in the development of an advertising man.

4. The first stage, I believe, is when he sees adver-tising as a form of communication, and sees its place in relation to all other elements of communication. We think of advertising as a force that makes people want to have something better than what they have now, makes them want to enjoy a better standard of living. It is, but advertising does not work in a vacuum. As much as by advertising, people are also influenced by what they see in the movies, by what they read in books, by the editorial content of magazines and newspapers, by the program content of television and radio. They are influenced by the theatre and the church, and by what they see when driving around in their automobiles—or observing what their neighbors have.

5. I think the second stage of an advertising man's development is when he sees advertising in relation to all the other factors of marketing—when he realizes that advertising cannot work at peak efficiency unless a product is properly distributed and merchandised. In other words, advertising must be integrated with all the processes that make the product available to the consumer. But actually, this is so much not a matter of linking up a host of independent, separately planned

selling functions, as it is a matter of putting into a marketing operation that extra something an athlete has when they say his muscles are coordinated, synchronized and timed to attain the goal.

6. I believe the third stage of development comes when an advertising man can distinguish between a strong quiet voice and shouting—between being skillful and making noise. No doubt we are *all* tempted nowadays to shout louder and make more superlative claims than the next fellow. The great volume of advertising now directed at consumers could well suggest that unless we shout we may not be heard at all. But that suggestion is misleading. Would you be more apt to listen to a salesman who exaggerates and screams all over the place—or to one who presents you with an interesting and believable story? And in the same vein, this brings to mind the remark of a showman who I think has a greater touch with humankind than anyone I've ever met. Apropos of interesting an audience, he said to me: "Anyone can tell a dirty story, but it takes *skill* to entertain.

7. His next stage of development is when an advertising man realizes that the public's belief in advertising is advertising's greatest asset. This is also when he realizes that the most effective advertising is advertising which people can understand and believe.

8. I think that every advertising man (and this includes women) should look at every advertisement he or she creates or approves, and then give an honest answer to this question: "Would I believe this advertisement enough to make me want to buy the product?"

9. It is difficult for me to see how an advertising man who understands people could ever take the view that although he could not believe the advertisement, the public will be taken in by it.

If he really understood people—the public—he'd know he is one of them and the others are no different than he is.

10. But believability is not always a matter of honesty. It is often a matter of credibility, and what you say can be credible if you talk in terms of the experience of those to whom you are talking. Only a few years ago a trip to the moon was an incredible thing —today it is credible.

I can't name the final stage in an advertising man's development because, as I said in the early part of this document, an advertising man never ceases developing. Even if I went to twenty stages, there could still be more.

11. So I'll conclude with what I think is probably the most important stage of development. It is this. It is when an advertising man has acquired enough experience so that he, within himself, has the courage of his convictions— when he can look at an advertisement or a campaign and say with conviction, "I know this is good," and state why he thinks so. But this is definitely not a matter of "knowing it all," for a part of courage is the recognition that no matter how much you now about advertising, there is till more to learn.

12. Within the whole area of advertising activity, only a small art is measurable. Most of the dimensions are intangible and hence immeasurable. That is why skilled judgment is essential. This is easy to understand if you think of advertising in terms of its ultimate objective— i.e., molding people's opinions and attitudes—and not just in terms of administering the tools and mechanics of advertising.

13. For example, take advertising media. We get to thinking about advertising media as if they were mechanical vehicles which tote advertisements into the more

desirable households atso much per thousand. But mere numbers are inanimate, and people are not inanimate.

14. First of all, an advertising medium must be a newspaper or a magazine or a TV show into which an editor or showman has breathed the breath of life—making it something of living interest to people. An editor calls these people circulation; a showman calls them audience; we call them markets. But they are all the same people—living, pulsating human beings—responsive but unpredictable.

15. A publisher I know had the courage to rightly answer an advertiser who asked him if he had any evidence that his magazine "moved goods." He said that was not the function of his magazine; the magazine's function was to move minds. He was right. The commodity we deal in is people's minds. You have to move minds before you have a successful publication, and similarly you have to move minds before you have successful advertising.

16. In view of the increasing importance that mar-keting places on research, these comments would not be complete without reference to the subject. I believe that research is our single most useful tool, and hence advice on its use is appropriate. Here is the advice. It is very simple. Never forget that a man's reach should exceed his grasp. So, research man to learn what man wants, but then give him something better than he wants. This goes for baked beans or television shows. Create something better than he has and offer it to him. That is the best way to win his regard.

17. The very nature of advertising calls for innovation. And innovation calls for imagination, and equally calls for courage. On that premise I can tell you what I believe are the qualifications for an advertising man. It is a combination of being adventurous and being cautious— having courage to enter unexplored areas and do

things in a new way, along with a willingness to use all the safety devices which are at your disposal and which will help to assure you of a happy outcome to your adventure.

18. And my last word of advice—at every opportunity expose yourself to other advertising people, especially those whom you regard as better advertising men than you regard yourself. Above all, keep exposing yourself to people.

Frederic R. Gamble

F rederic R. Gamble was graduated magna cum laude from Knox College in 1920, and as a Rhodes Scholar received a B.A. degree from Oxford University in 1922 and an M.A. degree in 1931. Knox also gave him an honorary LL.D. in 1957. After six years in Chicago in investment banking and as representative of the *Saturday Evening Post,* he joined the American Association of Advertising in 1929 as Executive Secretary. He was made Managing Director of the Association in 1940 and has been President since 1944.

More Than Twenty Things I Have Learned in More Than Twenty Years in Advertising

Frederic R. Gamble

1. In my early days as an advertising manager, I remember developing with our agency what I thought was a very fine ad. Its headline was the single word, "Milestones." To my chagrin some people pronounced it "my-less-toe-knees," as if it were a Greek word.

   MORAL: Use simple words that cannot be misunderstood or so easily mispronounced.

2. At about the same time we developed a series of ads, each one making a special point about the bonds we were advertising. We labeled the ads No. i of a series, No. 2 of a series, etc. They were not successful as far as we were able to judge. Dealing with only one of our selling points was an incomplete story. From that I learned that each ad should be self-supporting, should tell the whole story. I never had anything to do with a series again.

3. As a young magazine salesman, I had occasion to see an advertiser about a claim of error. I've forgotten

now whether it was poor printing or some other mistake. At any rate, I was telling him how serious this was and it was growing larger and larger in his mind. He said, "Let's go over to the factory next door and talk with my partner." On the way over through the snow, my sales manager who was with me whispered to me, "Play it down, minimize it." So when we arrived at the other end, I started talking about how slight this was and how little it meant. At first our customer gasped a little but pretty soon he and his partner agreed with us that it was a minor matter after all, and our job was done.

4. Another sales principle I learned about the same time was the one I call, "If you get out on a limb, you don't always have o climb all the way back on the same limb. Jump over to another one."

5. Sons in the father's business in most parts of advertising usually create a problem. For a good many years I have been convinced that the son should ordinarily start some place else and make a name for himself— prove his worth—before he comes back to the father's organization. Where this has happened, I believe the sons have been successful. Where it has not been done, sometimes the sons have and sometimes they have not.

6. Getting young men to go to college. A good friend of mine once asked me to talk with his son who had made up his mind that he didn't want to go to college. I did my best and got exactly nowhere with the young man who, without college, has turned out to be a very successful businessman as his father was before him. But I'm still trying. Even today I'm supplying some material to the Sergeant of our State Police for his son who thinks he doesn't want to go to college. As yet, I don't know the answer to that one.

Maybe young people who don't want to go to college shouldn't go. If college is not looked upon by them as an opportunity, they probably won't do very much with it.

7. One of the earliest lessons to learn in the advertising agency business is that hiring individuals who control accounts is not a sound way to build an advertising agency. This so-called vest-pocket account too often goes out with the man still wearing his vest.

8. On the most serious note I can sound, of all these items I select, the most important is the need of creating and maintaining confidence. It seems to me that this applies to every business job, to every salesman who wants to have continuing customers—not just one-time sales— and it applies especially to an association.

I've spent most of my business life, it seems to me, making decisions on the basis of what will create the greatest confidence in our organization and me, and I believe that this pays off in a very large and important way.

I think it's the most important single thing in business.

9. From time to time, people in the advertising business are out of jobs, quite often through no fault of their own. This can be a difficult experience for an individual and if it goes along for a long time, a person can easily get depressed, especially if he doesn't have fairly substantial reserves.

Over the years I have talked with scores of people about the problem of finding jobs and have learned that the most important point to make with them is that they have a personal marketing problem. They should seek to find an employer who needs what they are able to supply. The problem is just that simple, and they should look upon themselves as the product for which they are seeking the best possible market. When they can deal with their problem that objectively, confidence comes back and usually within a very short time, they have some good news for themselves.

10. I'm reminded of a point in speechmaking that applies to other business contacts, and that I have long called "Don't apologize." To start off a speech with an apology is to me almost a sure way to ruin it. I think the same is true of most letters or sales presentations. If you have made some mistake, yes, by all means admit it, call it an error and issue a correction. There are places to apologize but certainly not at the beginning of a speech or a sales presentation.

11. Speaking of speeches, I think one of the most important things to find out is the time limit and then observe it strictly. If the whole program is running late and you can cut your material, then by all means cut it. I once saw that done by Doctor Slotemaker, Executive Vice President of KLM at a meeting in Naples; also by die late Ed Lloyd of A.C. Neilson who cut from about fifteen minutes to five when a previous speaker had run overtime.

Observing time limits is one of the most important things in running meetings. It is primarily the responsibility of the convention executive. We watch our timing very carefully. Sometimes I think we overdo it, but it's an important element in running a successful meeting.

12. If you ever have anything to do with planning business meetings, you may be interested in the idea of checklists, which we have used for a number of years.

Immediately after the meeting, never at the meeting itself, we send to those who attended (and only to our members, not to guests) checklists asking them to evaluate the speakers and various parts of the program, to tell us whether they consider them Excellent, Good, Neutral or Poor, and to give us their suggestions as to whether there was too much or too little of anything. We ask for suggestions for future meetings, too.

Following is the sort of brief note which accompanies the checklist and asks the member to help the cause along by answering:

'Won't you please give us your frank comments on the _____ Meeting, for the guidance of those who will plan next year's meeting?

"Use the attached checklist, or write us if you prefer.

"Don't hesitate to make critical comments, since these will be most useful and will not be identified beyond Headquarters.

"If your lady accompanied you, a checklist for the Ladies' Program is also enclosed, for her comments.

"Thank you very much for your help."

13. The results are tabulated, including the suggestions, and when the committee meets to plan the next year's meeting, its members have the advantage of reviewing the last year or two, seeing what was done, what people liked and what they didn't like and what their suggestions are for the future.

It has been an invaluable tool in helping us to improve our meetings and is much to be preferred to the gathering of a program-planning group who start without guidance, pulling their ideas for a meeting out of the blue.

Some have thought to improve on this method by giving out checklists at the meeting itself. This doesn't work ordinarily because people hesitate at the time to rate anybody low. They do a much better job of appraising a program when they get back to their own offices a few days afterward than in the meeting itself.

14. Speaking of meetings, what you do about visuals can make the difference between a good attractive meeting and one which gives the impression of being badly run.

    All slides should be bright, should be large enough to be seen by everyone.

    Simplify and light them properly. Keep the slide material succinct and clear. Be sure the projection equipment is clean, too?

15. It is not uncommon at meetings of committees and boards to have a considerable amount of material supplied at his place for each of the participants. If you want a good, free-flowing discussion, you will get more of it, in my experience, by limiting the material you supply.

    If the participants feel that there is a great deal of undigested material in front of them, they will be much less ready to take part in the discussion. If they feel they grasp fully everything they have been supplied with, they will tend to speak more freely.

16. Present whatever factual material there is first, so that all those in the meeting will feel they are on the same basis and can speak freely.

    It will inhibit discussion if there is any indication that anyone in the group possesses information or knowledge that is not available to everyone else and is likely to undercut somebody after he has spoken.

17. Sound finances. Many associations that I have had something to do with (not our own, fortunately) have spent more time on finances than any other subject. For an association to do its best work, I think you have to

solve the financial problem first so that you can then spend most of your members' time and your staff's time on the problems of the industry you represent.

It seems a great pity to have to continue to spend valuable time of industry members on problems of financing the association instead of the true problems of the industry.

18. Another common association problem is how to deal with differences between members—geographical, size, and other differences.

The only solution I have ever found for this is to treat all alike. Set policies which will not penalize any member by his geographical location. The opposite of this is to try to put each member on an individually paying basis. In my experience, this won't work.

19. Good administration follows policy to the letter.

Some administrators tend to try to make policy, which is wrong; others tend not to follow it if they are unsympathetic with it.

It should be possible always to draw the line clearly between policy decisions and administrative decisions. Once the policy decisions are made, a good administration will adhere strictly to them, and enthusiastically, too!

20. When an organization grows beyond one executive or a very small group, the chief executive finds it necessary to delegate, and this means if you're going to get real value out of an organization that you must really delegate.

You must follow up, of course, to see that things are done, how they are done and perhaps to suggest how they might be done better, but don't interfere within the area you have delegated.

Give the officer to whom you have delegated responsibility full authority within that area. How can you hold him responsible if you don't let him run his own section or department?

21. Finally, there are some written materials to which it pays to devote enormous amounts of time editing and re-editing; others —well, you can get through your day's work only by letting some things go out that aren't fully up to standard or even contain minor errors.

You can do the latter in the case of some letters, but not, of course, vitally important letters.

Bulletins, newsletters and other material which are to be widely circulated need the most careful editing.

There are a great many fine careful people in business who give exactly the same kind of attention to every problem and every job that comes along.

One of the problems in training people to increase their capacity is to get them to discriminate between the sort of thing on which they should put endless amounts of time, to come as close as possible to perfection, and other things where they need to do just a good commercial job in order to finish the day's business.

Bernice Fitz-Gibbon

Bernice Fitz-Gibbon, after graduating from the University of Wisconsin, became a newspaper reporter on the *Rockford Morning Star,* joining the *Rockford Register-Gazette* in 1921. At Marshall Field's, Chicago, she had her first training and experience in retail advertising. Moving to Macy's, she created "It's smart to be thrifty." Advertising Director of Wanamaker's was next. Then at Gimbels, she put the "Nobody but nobody" slogan on the map.

She now heads her own consulting organization.

20 Things I've Learned in 20 Years

Bernie Fitz-Gibbon

1. Advertising is a craft, and a craft can be learned. You can make yourself into an engineer. You can make yourself into a lawyer. Can you make yourself into a novelist or a poet or a playwright? I suspect not. But I do believe that you can make yourself into a creditable advertising writer, because advertising writing does not require that rare kind of talent that sustained writing requires. Shaw's advice to would-be writers (somebody said that it was given off the top of his head, but even the top of Shaw's head was better than other people's whole heads) was this: "Write a thousand words a day for the next five years. A man learns to skate by staggering about and making a fool out of himself."

2. Don't worry too much if, when you start, you cannot think of anything startlingly new or original to put down. They say that there is no such thing as a really new melody—that there has been a standing offer in Vienna of $25,000 to anyone who can write eight bars of original

music. The offer has been up for decades. Thousands of compositions have been submitted, but every single one has been traced back to some old melody.

3. I get pretty sick of those sober pontifical denunciations of advertising copy that is fresh, bright, light, clever, juicy, exciting, and witty. I think it's a case of sour grapes. The critics criticize clever ads because they are not clever enough to write clever ads.

4. A good ad should be good reading. It should be "unlaydown-able." It should also be very "pickupable." You've heard about the books that "you just can't put down." But you can't lay them down until you pick them up. You can't be interested until something stops you or stirs you or tickles your fancy. No ad is ever sought out and read by anybody except die person who wrote it or the one who paid for it. It must cut across the reader's complacency and rivet his attention. My motto, with a bow to Hilaire Belloc, has always been: "When I am dead, let only this be said: 'Her sins were scarlet but her ads were read!'"

5. Get up early in the morning. The founder of Wellesley once said that he'd rather have one calico girl than two velvet girls. So would I. Calico carries the connotation of a lively, hard working, fast-moving doer. Velvet stirs up a vision of a dilettante languidly hovering over a brandy Alexander at four o'clock any afternoon.

6. The materials which a copywriter uses are words. His tools area Thesaurus and a large, unabridged dictionary. A good copy writer should actually read the dictionary— go through it in the evenings as if it were what it is, an interesting book.

7. Sharpen your powers of observation. Learn to look at a thing as if you had never seen it before in your life. As

I look back over thirty years of writing advertising and thirty years of helping young people and middle-aged people and older people break into advertising, I really believe that the one common denominator among the successful ones has been this sense of wonder - this holy curiosity. I once hired a young cub, right out of college (he went on to become editor of *Esquire)* just because he said, "A horse looks like a violin from above." How did he know? He had climbed up in the rafters of the barn and looked down. And a horse *does* look like a violin from above.

8. Even if your diploma came from 'way back near the tail of the sheep, or even if you never finished the eighth grade, you can still be the possessor of a rich, wide, tremendous vocabulary. Investigators eager to test captains of industry who had scanty formal educations approached one tycoon who refused to take the test. He said, "Frankly, I'm scared. I quit school after the fourth grade. I couldn't have much of a vocabulary. I don't want you to show me up before all these smart college fellers that work for me." He was finally persuaded to take die test, along with the Ph.D's in his company, and of course he came out 'way on top.

9. Make it your business to acquire good taste. We were all born with no taste—other than the taste in our mouths. The person who gets ahead makes a steady day-by-day effort to understand what is beyond him. He keeps looking at things and listening to things and tasting things that at first don't appeal to him. Eventually, his tastes change and he catches up with what used to be beyond him.

10. Sometimes the smartest thing you can do is to turn a com- plete about-face and offer something in total opposition to a trend. Several years ago doll manufacturers were

breaking their necks to produce dolls that did everything but scrub the kitchen sink. In turn, we were breaking our necks to sell each new wonder as it came along. One day, grown giddy with these attempts at verisimilitude, we stopped to reflect and were struck with an idea. We went instantly to designer Mme. Alexander of the Alexander Doll Company. Curiously enough, (perhaps not so curiously, since it is a fact that the identical idea often pops up simultaneously in different minds), we were thinking along the same lines. Mme. Alexander had already decided to bring out a simple old-fashioned doll. So we put our ideas together, and the doll was advertised this way: "Meet Miss Flora McFlimsey, who positively *won't* walk, won't talk, won't burp, won't coo, won't wet." The copy went on to declare: "Miss Flora McFlimsey is *not* the latest mechanical jerk in the doll business. She is, wonder of wonders, simply an exquisitely beautiful doll, meant simply to be loved. That is to say, she does *not* open her little yap or wail for mama or suck her thumb or sob real tears or dampen her didy or roller skate or bat her eyes or up-chuck. Her little heart doesn't tick-tock; she doesn't even go to sleep. She is merely a winsome model of old-fashioned Victorian decorum." Well. While all the manufacturers of doll-automatons watched in horror, we sold hundreds and hundreds of dolls from one teensy ad, and even had one order from the Union of South Africa, where the *New York Times'* circulation is not notably high.

11. Don't think you're tired. Because you are really not, you know. Remember, mental work is never tiring. And it has been proven that even after hours of hard physical labor, muscle energy can be restored in about twenty minutes. Fatigue, of any kind, is usually boredom.

12. Making money is easy. Because you won't be making much money unless you are having a whale of a lot

of fun doing what you are doing. Which will be called work. But if you are having fun, you are not working hard. You're working easy. The surest way to make money is to get into something that you like so much you would do it even if you weren't being paid at all. At least, you'd want to do it. Maybe you couldn't afford actually to work for nothing. But you should feel, "All this—and money too—here I am having a barrel of fun—and getting paid *too.*"

13. Only the unfrantic succeed. You can be ambitious— but it must be a relaxed ambition. You must cultivate the "relaxed grasp." You must sit loosely in the saddle. You must appear to be almost drifting—you can drift energetically. You must not be a bundle of nerves. You must be a bundle of calm. You mustn't have a Messianic gleam in your eye. A man with a mission is bad. A miss with a mission is awful.

14. Especially in department store copy writing, a person may rocket to fame practically overnight. That is because in a retail advertising department, there is no anonymity. In an advertising agency, there are so many fingers in the pie that it is hard to pin down the writer of any particular piece. Department store writers, whose work appears mainly in newspapers, work much more quickly—there's usually no more than two weeks before the ad is planned and its appearance in the paper. I have known young cubs who have been in the department less than six months to produce such fresh startling headline and editorial copy that people all over New York were asking, "Who wrote that terrific ad for Wanamaker's that ran in today's *Herald Tribune?*" Even though the policy of the advertising department is always to say, "It was the work of the department—we do not give out individual names"—by nightfall scores of people would know it was actually little Mary Ellen McGillicuddy who wrote it.

15. Don't ask "Where will I go to find out?" A famous professor once startled his students by saying: "I know nothing; but, gentlemen, I have learned how to find out anything I might want to know." The purpose of an education is to teach sources and channels of information, not to file a lot of facts to be memorized.

16. You'll never get anywhere without a good healthy respect for yourself. The most well-adjusted and successful people always have affection for themselves. There is none of the groveling "Oh, but you—you are a Prince and I—I am only a commoner" attitude that seems to be trying to say, "See how modest I am about my accomplishments." But it's a phony cover up. A really humble person is also frankly proud of an honest accomplishment.

17. Youth ought to take chances. I am always a little depressed to find young people right out of college worried about security, inquiring about old age pensions and insurance plans. Some of the best writing cubs that I have ever hired have been ones that lit out for Europe the day after graduation with a few hundred dollars of gift graduation money. They managed, with a little help from home, to make their way as nursemaids or waitresses or typists. They didn't worry about all the Johnnies-on-the-spot grabbing up all the good openings before they got back. They came into the office in late November with paragraphs in their fists so full of the freshness and abandon of youth that one couldn't resist hiring them.

18. Creativeness often consists of merely turning up what is there already. Charles Helser, one of the nation's best merchandisers, once looked perceptively at a manufacturer's immense stock of pewter porringers for babies. "Porringers are out of date," the manufacturer

murmured sadly to Charles in a reminiscent tone as the two of them were passing the porringer mountain one day. "And if they weren't—what could be more old-fashioned than this early American design?" Charles looked hard at the porringers and made a deal. The maker could hardly believe his ears—not that the price was so high (it was rock bottom) but that a smart merchant could fall for porringers at all. Now the usual mark-up that a store tacks onto its merchandise is 40%. Charles marked up his porringers over 55%, and had a sellout on the first ad! He advertised them not as porringers but as ash trays. What was his principal selling point? He played up the authentic old-fashioned early American design.

19. When it comes to money—don't give it a thought! Take no care of the things of the morrow. Don't ask for a raise—at least during die first semester. You should enjoy your job so much that you can hardly stand it. As I have said, the quickest way to make money is to be sure to get into something that you like so much that you would do it even if you weren't being paid any thing at all. I have watched that over the years—and great guns, how the money rolls in. (Of course, I am speaking of business, fashion, merchandising, styling, advertising, and promotional lines—certainly not of school teaching.)

Now you probably won't believe a word of this but it is true that when you like what you are doing so much that the prize, the trophy, die stipend, the weekly salary check dims in interest, the old couplet holds:

> Not the quarry *but the chase*
>
> Not the trophy *lout the race.*

20. Don't brag about what you cannot do. This is a curious trait of many people, young and old. Ralph Waldo Emerson noted it long ago. He said: "If I cannot brag of knowing something, then at least I can brag of *not* knowing it." Don't say that you have a poor memory, or execrable handwriting, or that you can't master detail, or that your hands are all thumbs. You'll be found out soon enough.

Dan Goldstein

D an Goldstein is Vice President of Schenley Distillers, Inc. He is Director of Merchandising and Sales Promotion and also heads the company's creative research and development operations. He attended the University of Texas where he majored in journalism and advertising. Since joining Schenley in 1936, Mr. Goldstein has earned a national reputation as an expert in the fields of advertising, merchandising and sales promotion. His broad, outstanding achievements with Schenley sales administration make him a recognized authority. Recently he was awarded the coveted Edgar . . . the industry's equivalent of Hollywood's Oscar . . . for helping to stimulate business through creative thinking.

20 Tips and Checklists for Beginners

Dan Goldstein

1. GET OUT BEFORE IT'S TOO LATE!

To you who are just coming into the field of marketing, advertising, merchandising and sales promotion, I say "Welcome!"

However, if you're coming into this business only because of the impression you got from reading *The Hucksters* or some other fictionalized version of Madison Avenue life, my recommendation to you, simply and honestly, is—don't! If you're looking for the glamour of the Ivory Tower, if you want the ease of the two-and-a-half-hour lunch period and if you need the excitement of the "three martini" cocktail hour, I say, "Get out; get out before it's too late!"

If, however, you have the urge, if you have creative drive and guts, I say, "Look behind the glittering facade of the advertising business. Then—if you're not frightened when you find more work than glamour—take off your coat and go to work. We need you!"

Advertising is truly a field of long hours, of blood, sweat and tears. It's fraught with frustration, aggravation and heartache! But it's also a field of tremendous rewards in money, satisfaction and creative release for those who make the grade. And it's been my experience that those who do make the grade are the ones who realize the tremendous social responsibility they accept when they go into advertising and marketing.

Actually, it is you, the advertising and marketing man and woman, whose ideas and whose execution of those ideas keep the factories humming.

It is to you—and you alone in the last analysis—that the men and women in the factories look for steady employment. It is to you that the worker on the farm, the freight handler, the people who supply the raw materials, the fabricator of the finished product, the wholesaler, the salesman and even the retailer look for their very livelihood.

All this is true because it is you . . . yes, you . . . who actually creates the market for their produce.

It is you who designs the package, who thinks up the advertising campaign and executes the master marketing plan. It is you who eases, forces, pushes, cajoles or dynamites the finished product from the manufacturer, through the distributor, to the retailer and through him to the ultimate consumer.

Yes, in your hands, in your eyes, and, most important of all ... in your imagination . . . rests the economic security and future of this country. If you falter, the whole chain of production and distribution falters.

So get in with all your heart and imagination—or get out before it's too late!

2. NEVER SPEND MONEY . . . "INVEST IT"!

As long as you are in this business, never, never, never look at money or talk about money spent on good advertising as an expense. It isn't expenditure—it's an *investment!*

And it's a damn good one, too!

When you talk to a client—or if you are the client, when you talk to your agency—you must examine, plan and spend every single advertising and sales promotion dollar as carefully as you would examine, plan and buy a properly balanced portfolio of stocks for yourself!

If you remember, from the beginning, to handle your ever advertising budgets on this investment basis, you will find that advertising has a definite cumulative value. Yes, and it has a cash value, too!

Any lawyer or accountant will tell you that consumer acceptance and consumer demand are salable assets. They are like cash in the bank. Whenever a business is sold, the greater the good will, the greater the price! And what is good will but the consumer's opinion, his purchasing record and his current going rate of usage of the product? All of these, if the product represents honest value, are the results of advertising and merchandising dollars not just spent—but well invested—through the years.

Let's examine this a step further. The product image which the consumer learns to remember, to look for and to ask for is much more than just words or pictures.

If used consistently and intelligently, a great slogan, a memorable trade mark, a distinctive logotype or a trade character like Schenley's *Mr. I. W. Harper* or Philip Morris' *Johnny* become real properties. They are as real and as tangible as the factories, the warehouse, the machinery, and the products themselves!

Money invested in developing advertising properties is like money invested in developing plants and machinery. It pays dividends. But remember both are perishable! Neglect a plant and it becomes rusty and worthless; neglect an advertising idea or bastardize it through needless change, and it is soon forgotten!

Once you have created—or had created for you—a great advertising property, protect that property! Nurture it, build it, develop it, and then

USE IT!

USE IT!

USE IT!

3. MERCHANDISE YOUR ADVERTISING!

Merchandising the advertising is very much like the weather. Everybody talks about it, but no one does much about it either.

It's true that your advertising is directed at the consumer but why keep it a secret from your sales force? Why surprise them with the schedule when it breaks?

And what about the retailer? Let him know about it in advance so he can tie into it—to his benefit and yours—by displaying and featuring your product when the advertising runs!

Details of the schedules in every medium and reprints of the ads themselves sent out in advance—repeat, in advance—are powerful sales weapons in the hands of a properly oriented sales organization. That goes for your own and for your distributors' sales organizations as well.

And don't just send out reprints in the usual drab, routine manner. Do it with enthusiasm! Do it with drama! Do it with color and excitement!

Here are a few suggestions. Use them; even more important, develop a library of merchandising ideas of your own!

1) Send schedules and reprints to the salesman's home!

2) Put them in a folder that will fit his brief case or order pad. Make them easy for the salesman to use!

3) Make the folder cover a "teaser." Make it fun for the salesman to show and fun for the retailers to read or listen to!

4) Send two copies of magazines carrying your copy to the sales men's homes. Mark one for "The wife to read," and one for "The husband to merchandise."

5) Put gummed strips on reprints so they can be posted on retailers' windows, cash registers, shelves and displays.

6) When you make reprints, leave a blank space at the bottom for the retailer to print his own name.

7) Give your distributor a bundle of reprints to put into every broken case he sends to the retailer.

8) He can use them as inserts with invoices and correspondence.

9) Run a "Do you know your advertising schedules" contest. Every week have a secretary in the home office draw three names out of a hat. Call long distance and if the salesman knows without referring to the schedule when the next ad is to run, or who the guest star on your next TV show will be, he wins a portable TV set or a case of Schenley Reserve!

10) Hey! How about the same type contest for retailers?

11) Have the local newspapers call 100 key accounts to tell them your schedule is running on such and such a date. Get the local TV and radio stations to do the

same. They are all anxious to cooperate! (They are? Well, most are!)

12) Send marked newspapers to retailers the day the ad runs. Have a ribbon tied around the outside with a card saying: "See YOUR Ad on page 22." Then have your product ad circled in red crayon or ink. If the retailer sees it and displays it, it truly becomes *his* advertisement too!

4. ICH KENNE MEIN VOLK

In the old days a marketing man who could truthfully quote the German proverb, *"Ich kenne mein Volk,"* was in business. It means: "I know my people!" It refers, of course, to their mental processes and reactions.

Today, if that's all he knows, he'd starve to death in his office or in the market place!

Knowing your people, important as that facet still is, is no longer enough. Your knowledge of the market place must include places as well as people! And it must be local as well as national! It must cover local media and local problems. And your knowledge of local people has to include the same basic ingredients that are required in die lead of a fast reading newspaper story:

WHO?
WHAT?
WHY?
WHEN?
WHERE?

You've got to know WHO your customers and potential customers are; WHAT they're doing; WHY they're doing it; WHEN they're doing it... and most important. . . WHERE!

Populations are constantly shifting. Certain states are booming. Some cities are attracting young people; others, older people. Some industrial cities, army centers and factory sites are bulging with workers and ready spending money; others are drying up.

What about the annual baby crop? Each year 4,250,000 new customers are born! And what are *you* doing to cash in on the exciting and ever growing "leisure time" market?

Are you spending your advertising and sales dollars where the biggest potential is? Are you fishing where the fish are?

And what about floods, blizzards, strikes, layoffs? Are you trying to sell people who haven't got the money to buy, or if they do have the money, who can't get to the stores? Are you advertising in papers that can't be delivered? Does the outdoor company owe you a refund for billboards that were washed away and not replaced for two months? Has a severe freeze cracked and chipped the paint on your outdoor advertisement to the point where it is unsightly and needs a repainting?

All of these marketing factors, and many, many more, influence whether or not you will run advertising! And if you do run, what kind of copy will it be? Short range? Long range? Public service?

Keep yourself posted. Keep all of the pertinent marketing facts at your fingertips. Be sure the facts are correct—*and wp to date.*

Remember the old proverb: Old truths are useless facts; They do not last any better than fish!

Do you have any dead fish at your finger tips?

5. A GRAVE OR A RUT?

Whenever you attack a problem that offers unusual resistance and doesn't seem solvable by your usual approaches, I strongly suggest that you think about . . . and actually work the famous old

Nine Circle problem. It was originally created as a test for perceptual blocks against creativity, but it also helps unfreeze your thinking.

Here's how it works! Draw nine circles forming a perfect square like this:

```
0       0       0

0       0       0

0       0       0
```

The problem is to take a pencil and draw a line through all nine of the circles. You must do it with only four continuous straight lines, *and without lifting your pencil from the paper.*

Try it several ways:

```
0       0       0              0       0       0

0       0       0              0       0       0

0       0       0              0       0       0
```

Still having trouble?

The key to solving this problem, like most difficult marketing problems, lies not in the problem itself. . but in the way you approach it!

If you will re-examine it, you will find that the statement of the problem limits only *what* you do, *not how you do it!* It does *not limit the boundaries* of your thinking. It doesn't say where the line should start. And it doesn't say where it should stop. That's up to you.

Follow the arrow in the next illustration and you'll see how easy it really is, if you carry the line, and your thinking *beyond* where you stopped it!

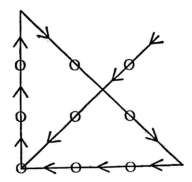

The object lesson here is that you must throw off the shackles that restrict your thinking. You must push back the borders of what you think you can do, and, even more important, what you think you *should* do. Push back . . . yes, *actually change the starting and stopping points of your thinking.*

The solution to many a difficult problem you will face lies merely in approaching it with a fresh point of view, unfettered by slavish devotion to what has been done before!

Don't follow the usual pattern. Break out! Break free of the chain of mediocre thinking and routine solutions. Get out of the rut because the only difference between a rut and a grave are the dimensions.

I refuse to be buried alive! How about you?

6. A HOUSE DIVIDED AGAINST ITSELF!

The old truism that "a house divided against itself cannot stand" is even truer of our business than of politics! Time after time, as both an agency man and a client, I have seen corporate structures, large and small alike, where the Sales Department, the Advertising

Department and the Merchandising Departments insisted on operating as separate entities.

In spite of corporate policy that dictated that they should work together, in spite of management engineers who proved they had to work together, and in spite of carefully drawn organization charts that showed them how to work together . . . they didn't!

Each, jealous of its own prerogatives, was vying for Top Management's approval, jockeying for control and operating independently of the others.

The results were always deadly to the product being sold, disastrous for the personnel and costly for the company.

My advice to you is never let yourself get "sucked" into a situation like this. Even if you are "with" the winner, you'll find you have won a Pyrrhic victory. You may win the argument but you'll lose the sale. And sooner or later you'll lose your job.

You are an advertising man, not a politician!

Dedicate yourself, whether you are the agency man or the client, to integrating the company's advertising, merchandising and sales program. They are one and the same!

A house divided against itself cannot stand. It must fall!

Don't be under it!

7. FIND YOUR CREATIVE CATALYST . . . AND SCHEDULE IT!

The fastest way to get results in creative thinking is to find by trial and error just what is the best creative climate for you.

Some people do their best thinking and problem solving by working alone. Some think best in the morning, some at night, some in the shower, some while shaving, some in church, and others while walking to work, and others in the subway! Still others think best in their office with the phone shut off and their feet on the desk!

Some creators find they are stimulated to better thinking if they attack the problem with a pencil and paper in their hands, even if they are not artists. They just doodle or scratch, write or draw until the spark hits them. Others simply wrap their legs around a typewriter table and just start banging away.

I have also found, through the years, that many idea men find their most effective catalyst to be *other people!* Many a great idea is developed in either a brainstorm session or an informal bull session, or just talking about the problem with an associate. It can be an ad director, a copy writer, a salesman, a client, your wife or your secretary!

The important thing is not how you get your ideas but *how often* you get them.

If one of these techniques doesn't work, try another. Try them all! Try new ones, too, until you find the one which stimulates you most. Then use it! Sometimes you'll find a combination of methods the most productive. First try solo thinking. Then if the idea or plan is incomplete ... or doesn't jell . . . talk it out with some one else. Talk it out with one person or a group-but only if they are compatible and if they have been *oriented not to stifle fresh -points of view!* Always set up your discussion in two definite stages. The first half of the meeting must be devoted entirely to the creative development of the ideas; the second half should be used for the evaluation of the ideas.

Regardless of how you do your creative thinking or when, learn to schedule it. And do some every day! You'll find it soon gets to be a habit, a happy habit, and a profitable one too!

8. WHAT HAVE YOU GOT FOR TOMORROW?

There is an old proverb that says: "No man ever enters the same river twice." This is true because the water never stands still. It keeps flowing on, and each time he enters it, he actually enters a fresh river.

This advertising business is like a frothing and powerful river that cannot and should not be stopped! Every day is a new day. Every day presents a new challenge and a host of new problems that must be solved because every day there is more merchandise produced and more services available that must be sold. This ceaseless, ever-growing flood of marketable goods constantly needs new ideas, new programs and new plans. It is a business that eats up ideas faster than television eats up a comedian's library of jokes.

Never stop thinking!

Never stop planning!

And just as important, never stop making notes! Whenever and wherever you get an idea, or even a fragment of a thought, *write it down!* Never be without a notebook in your pocket on the train, in your office or in your home. Yes, even in bed! Don't think you can remember your "hot flashes" and ideas and then document them later. You can't! Nobody can!

After you've documented and roughly illustrated your idea, use it or file it. Create your own idea library and review it often! Its contents are an important part of your stock in trade.

An inventory of ready, usable ideas is just as important as the ability to create new ones.

For years, I have reminded myself of the daily need for new ideas with a thought provoker in the form of a printed card on my door. It is the last thing I see when I leave my office at night. It is a sign which asks the question which you must also ask yourself every night from now on: WHAT HAVE YOU GOT FOR TOMORROW?

9. LET YOURSELF GO!

When you present a campaign, an idea or a budget, don't be afraid of the sound of your own voice!

Let yourself go!

Dramatize your presentation. Do it enthusiastically and force-fully. Your listener, be he client, boss, salesman or retailer, must respond to showmanship. I have seen and heard and made many presentations. Some were elaborate and costly; others were simple and inexpensive but they were just as effective!

I told one agency man that I had no time for a lot of sales talk or a lengthy presentation. He came in with the shortest, simplest, most inexpensive presentation I have ever seen! And it was the most dramatic!

He came into my office with only one ad. It was a single black-and-white layout. But it was in a folder . . . and it was covered with six sheets of white paper.

He opened the folder, and I was confronted with a blank white page of bond paper. He had accomplished his purpose! I expected to see a lot of printed words. The blank white page threw me off guard and focused my attention on what was to come. He made a few pertinent statements concerning the idea he was about to present and ripped off the first blank page. There was a second blank page! He did this five times, with a brilliant running commentary that was short, well thought out and to the point.

When he ripped off the fifth white page, there was the ad! By this time, he not only had my attention, but with it, the approval he wanted!

1O. BE NOT THE FIRST—BE NOT THE LAST!

You are in a business which, because it lives on new ideas, is constantly the target for people who are developing and selling new techniques.

You must keep an open mind to all new approaches and you must have the courage to pioneer a *good* idea. But the acid test of the value of a new idea or a different technique lies in the question:

"Is it better—or is it just different?"

If you have time to think an idea or a new technique through, to research it thoroughly, to project it properly and are willing to hang your hat on the results, then I agree with Farragut's philosophy of "Damn the torpedoes and full speed ahead!"

If, however, you and your associates have not done the necessary "agonizing appraisal and reappraisal," if you don't have sufficient facts on which to base your judgment, then I suggest you follow the poet Alexander Pope's admonition:

> Be not the first by whom the new are tried,
>
> Nor yet the last to lay the old aside!

11. BORROW! CHANGE! ADAPT! COMBINE!

Don't be discouraged if your first attempts at creative thinking don't bring the dramatic and exciting results you want. Creative men are not born; they are made.

And the best of them are self-made!

In creative thinking and creative problem solving, as in golf or tennis, practice makes perfect.

Here are some suggestions that may help you over the first rough spots. Until you have learned to develop new ideas of your own, bear in mind that creativity need not always mean invention. It doesn't even always mean coming up with a completely new and original idea. Why not start by coming up with a new application of an old idea? Why not change an existing idea by improving it? And why not combine two existing ideas, and thus create a completely new one?

Many a man in your shoes has launched his career ... or based his claim to fame ... on a new application of an old idea borrowed from a completely unrelated field, and then cleverly applied it to his own business.

12. YOUR MONEY AND MY REPUTATION!

In this business, you've got to have conviction—and you've got to have guts! The toughest sale I ever made was the result of my complete faith in the advertising program I was selling, and the guts to stake my future on it.

I made a presentation to the Chairman of the Board of one of America's largest and most successful corporations. The campaign I presented had been carefully thought out and researched. I presented it with a great deal of enthusiasm and conviction but, at the end of an hour, without much success.

The Chairman said: "I know you believe in what you are selling, but I just can't see it yet. You are not going to spend our money on this campaign."

The only answer I could think of in the heat of the excitement of presenting something I truly believed in was, "Mr. Chairman, I am risking your money but I am also risking my reputation! You have a lot of money but I have only one reputation! I have more at stake than you have! What do you say?"

The Chairman said, "O.K."

We ran the campaign and, thank the Lord, it produced the desired results.

13. WHAT THE EYE ADMIRES THE HEART DESIRES . . . AND THE CUSTOMER BUYS.

A well-rounded advertising or marketing man, like a well-rounded advertising program, must take into consideration all the facets of the problem as well as all of the available media.

Too many advertising men often forget the all-important point-of-sale material.

Unfortunately, you don't live in a world of your own. And the product you sell isn't sold in a world of its own. You and your product are doing business, are fighting for the consumer's attention and for his dollar in a viciously competitive, cut-throat, dog-eat-dog arena.

And that arena is the retail point of sale!

All of your ideas and all of your work either succeed brilliantly or fail miserably at the exact place, and at the precise moment that the customer puts his hand in his pocket!

Let's examine this.

Granted you have a great outdoor campaign. Your competitor has spectaculars, 24-sheets and painted bulletins too.

You have a powerful magazine campaign. Your competitors have one too.

Granted you have a big space (or small space) newspaper campaign. So do they.

You use T.D.I. They do too!

You have radio and/or TV. Well, your competition is in there, too.

You have wonderful window displays. Unfortunately, so do they.

Mr. Consumer riding on the train or in his car, bus or street car sees all of the outdoor advertising and car cards. When he reads his paper and magazine, he sees their ads as well as yours. When he walks into the store, he sees their window display as well as yours. So far, to a degree, everything is even. You and each of your competitors have loaded your sales guns, pointed the guns and made the consumer conscious of them. But the trigger has not been pulled. It won't be pulled; it can't be pulled . . . until the customer is inside the store!

That is the moment of decision!

The product that dominates the point of sale *makes* the sale because it dominates the consumer's imagination and his attention at the psychological time when he puts his hand in his pocket. That's the time when he is *able* to buy, *willing* to buy and *ready* to buy!

So always remember that, important as they are, your outdoor, your magazines, your newspaper, your television, your radio, your T.D.I., and your window displays are only the charge in your sales bomb.

Your point-of-sale material is the detonator!

14. USE MENTAL SPURS.

Even the most prolific idea men find some days harder than others to get their creative wheels in motion. Many use "stimulators" in the form of cards on their desks, signs on the walls or papers in their wallets. These quotations act as spurs on mental horsepower! Here are some of my favorites!

DON'T JUST SIT THERE . . .

THINK UP A WAY TO DO IT BETTER!

MAKE THINGS HAPPEN!

THERE IS NO DEFENSE . . . EXCEPT STUPIDITY . . .

AGAINST A NEW IDEA!

NO MAN'S MIND STRETCHED BY A NEW IDEA CAN EVER GO BACK TO ITS ORIGINAL DIMENSIONS[1].

MONEY IS WHAT YOU USE WHEN YOU RUN OUT OF IDEAS!

WHAT HAVE YOU THOUGHT UP TODAY?

ONE TORCH LIGHTS ANOTHER!

HE WHO NEVER EXPECTS TO FIND THE UNEXPECTED . . .

NEVER FINDS IT!

15. IT IS WHAT YOU SAY BUT It's ALSO *HOW* YOU SAY IT!

In advertising there is no question that what you say and when and where you say it is all-important. I would like to point out, however, that how you say it is important too! How you say it is the wedge that captures the consumer's attention and drives home the message.

I didn't learn this lesson from a great copy chief. And I didn't learn it from a great art director. Actually, I picked it up from an itinerant show card writer, whose only claim to fame was a fast speed-ball pen and an uncanny knowledge of how people would react to art treatment and typography. His lesson was quick and to the point. The word . .

STINK

written in bold black stud-horse gothic actually stinks. Its connotation is odoriferous and unpleasant. It is disgusting and nauseating.

Now, let's take a look at the same word—and the same "stink" —spelled in Old English like this . . .

The word somehow has lost its odor. Gone is the nausea and the unpleasant connotation. Actually, it seems to take on, merely by a simple change of typeface, a new dignity and almost a degree of social acceptance.

Did you say . . . **STINK?**

No, I said . . .

16. USE THE DYNAMIC CATALYST¹!

Whether you are a client or an account executive, you can't fight your competition with one hand tied behind your back. Don't try it! No matter what the boys in the copy department tell you, no matter what coverage the boys in the media department show you, and no matter what proof the boys in the research department give you . . . remember that *advertising cannot do the job alone.*

Taking for granted that the product, the packaging and the pricing are right, the successful marketing of that product depends on four basic ingredients:

1. Advertising

2. Sales Promotion

3. Sales Power

4. Coordination

These are like the legs of a four-legged stool. Just try sitting on this stool with three, two or even one of the legs missing! The laws of gravity and keen competition will land you flat on your round if you leave out any one of these four essentials.

No matter how great the idea, advertising dollars must lose their force unless they are spearheaded by integrated sales promotion material, and driven home by powerful sales effort!

Alone, neither advertising nor sales promotion nor sales power is complete. Alone, each is ineffectual. When combined, however, with proper coordination . . . which is the dynamic catalyst . . . they must create an irresistible force which can and does sweep all sales resistance from its path!

17. CHECK YOUR DISTRIBUTION!

My first big failure in advertising was the luckiest thing that ever happened to me. It cost me my job, but it taught me a lesson that I have never forgotten.

The idea was right. The ads in print media jumped off page. The commercials pounded home the message, and the campaign went over with a bang!

Yes, the operation was a success, but the patient died!

When the sales figures came in, or I should say did not come in, I knew something was wrong. And so did the client! I checked everything. All the pieces seemed to fall into place until my boss said: "I wonder if die product's distribution was as thorough as the advertising coverage?"

That's when I found out that my advertising world—and yours —is not confined to the four walls of the office, nor to the city limits of New York. I went on a barnstorming trip around the complete territory where the advertising campaign had run.

I didn't just visit our salesmen!

I didn't just visit our distributors!

I called on Mr. Retailer, the last *and most important* link in the channel of distribution to the consumer. That's when I learned that sometimes the distribution figures given by a Sales Department are, shall we say, over-optimistic!

I found we had done saturation advertising but, unfortunately, the Sales Department had done only infiltration distribution.

The lesson I learned was always to check the distribution— *before* you distribute the advertising check!

This brings up the old argument about which comes first— the chicken or the egg. Certainly you must take into consideration the competitive situation, the size of the market, the type of product and whether you're introducing a new product or driving an old one.

There are certain circumstances when advertising *before* distribution is not only called for but is absolutely necessary! Some products and some businesses are set up to get almost automatic introduction and distribution when a new item is ready for market. In such cases, advertising in advance or concurrently speeds the process along and is economically sound.

Other types of products, however, should be in distribution *before* the advertising breaks. In such cases, advertising in advance is costly and ineffectual. Why not use point-of-sale material with the placement of the product to keep the dealer happy, and even more important, to tell the customer your story until distribution is great enough to justify the advertising.

In either situation, when I talk about distribution, I'm not referring to token distribution. That won't do! Your advertising dollar is given a ten-fold impact when your product has thorough distribution, not only in depth and in quantity—*but also in all sizes!*

18. BUY ME! TRY ME! TAKE ME HOME!

Never assume that packaging is a thing apart from advertising, merchandising and sales promotion.

The package is what the shouting's all about! It's what you are marketing, advertising, merchandising and promoting! It's actually the "meat and bones" of your job.

If it's properly designed, and it's part of your job to be sure that it is, your package is far more than just a container. It's the most important selling tool you've got!

Here's a partial check list to ask yourself about the package you sell:

1)   Does it stand out on the shelf?

2)   Is it competitive?

a) In shape?

b) In size?

c) In labeling?

d) In finish?

e) In overall appearance?

3) Does it have eye appeal?

4) Does it have taste appeal?

5) Is your product name on the package easy to read?

6) Is your product name on the package in the same logotype you are using in your advertising?

7) If you have a symbol or trade character, is it on the front of the package? If not, how about the back?

8) Is your slogan on the package?

9) Does your package have "billboard display value"?

10) Is your package easy to handle?

11) Does your package in words or pictures tell your product story?

12) Does your package design reflect the quality and price of the product?

13) Are the proper colors used to depict the type of product you sell?

14) Are the right colors used to appeal to the type of customers you're after?

15) Does your package have all the necessary recipes or instructions to make it easy for the consumer to use?

16) Does your package encourage and suggest new uses for your product to broaden the base of your business?

17) Does your package stack well?

18) Is your package so well designed that the retailer is proud to recommend it?

19) Does your package have a distinct personality that stands out from the others and speaks with authority? Does it say proudly to the consumer: "Buy me ... try me ... take me home! You'll like me . . . and most important of all . . . I'll impress your family and your friends"?

Actually, if it is properly conceived, designed and executed, the greatest ad ever written is the label of your product! And the greatest sales promotion piece ever created is the package itself!

Remember, the package and the label are the only advertisements that the consumer pays money for, takes into his own home *and looks at every time he uses your product!*

19. TAKE IT OUT OF THE BASEMENT!

No matter how well designed your package is ... remember, it has to be seen to be bought! That's why package placement is just as important as package design!

Be sure your package is not only competitive in appearance, but also competitive in retailing position. It must be prominent and dominant at the point of sale.

Make it your business to see that it is! Do it by needling, by harassing and by demanding that your Sales Department and your distributors get the product properly displayed. Sales promotion material alone is not enough. Have the actual product with it whenever you can! And you usually can if you try hard enough!

So take your merchandise out of the basement!

Take it out from under the counters!

Get it on the floor stackings, in the bin displays, on the counters, on the backbars and on the shelf! And most important of all —when it's on the shelf . . . get your merchandise at the eye level because *eye level is buy level.*

And that's the level you are seeking!

20. USE YOUR HEAD!

Whether you're developing marketing plans, creating advertising campaigns, designing sales promotion programs or working as an account executive, your success will depend on and will grow in direct ratio to your fluency as a creative thinker and a creative problem solver.

If you're not doing any of these things and you want to, use your head! Remember that a good idea doesn't care who has it. And it doesn't care where it's been had!

It is my firm conviction that almost anyone can develop and improve his idea output. You too can train, stimulate and harness your imagination to do your bidding ... if you really want to!

You can do it by study and by practice. You can do it by learning to question, to observe and associate. You can do it by learning to challenge the obvious; by learning to be unafraid of ridicule and failure. And you can do it best by deliberately trying to be more creative!

While there is no one perfect formula or system for developing ideas and solving problems, most experts agree that the creative process includes some or all of the following six steps:

1) Clarify, define, pinpoint and actually state both the problem and the goal. Preferably, write them down on paper. Then

break the problem down to working size. If necessary, break it down into several problems. Strip away the extraneous.

2) Gather all of the available data and information on the problem.

3) Break down, inspect and analyze the pertinent information. Study its significance. What does it actually mean? What might it mean *if?*

4) Think up, pile up and document as many ideas and solutions as you can. Go after quantity. The more ideas you pile up, the better the chance of getting a good one.

5) Let your subconscious help. If you don't hit the idea you need, let up for a while. Work on something else, take a walk or sleep on it overnight.

6) Organize all the resultant ideas. Evaluate them. Test the most promising ones. Then develop the one that proves the best.

Of all the steps outlined above, number 4 ... thinking up a quantity of ideas . . . seems to cause the most trouble. This is true because most would-be creative people make the mistake of trying to be creative and critical at the same time. You can't be. You must learn to evaluate your ideas *after* you think them up— not while you're doing it! Learn to suspend judgment until you have a quantity of ideas to choose from and combine.

This important point is clarified in Friedrich von Schiller's advice to a friend who bemoaned his lack of creative power. Schiller wrote:

"The reason for your complaint lies; it seems to me, in the constraint which your intellect imposes upon your imagination. Here I will make an observation, and illustrate it by an allegory. Apparently, it is not good, and indeed it hinders the creative work of the mind, if the intellect examines too closely the ideas already pouring in, as it were, at the gates.

"Regarded in isolation, an idea may be quite insignificant, and venturesome in the extreme, but it may acquire importance from an idea which follows it; perhaps, in a certain collocation with other ideas, which may seem equally absurd, it may be capable of furnishing a very serviceable link.

"The intellect cannot judge all those ideas unless it can retain them until it has considered them in connection with these other ideas. In the case of a creative mind, it seems to me, the intellect has withdrawn its watchers from the gates, and the ideas rush in pell-mell, and only then does it review and inspect the multitude. You worthy critics, or whatever you may call yourselves, are ashamed or afraid of the momentary and passing madness which is found in all real creators, the longer or shorter duration of which distinguishes the thinking artist from the dreamer. Hence your complaints of unfruitfulness, *for you reject too soon and discriminate too severely.*"

Happy thinking!

Alden James

S enior Vice-President of Outdoor Advertising, Inc. Formerly Sales Manager o£ *This Week* Supplements. Author of a bestseller . . . *Careers in Advertising.*

The Practical Psychology of Success in Advertising

Allen James

There is a cliché which says we learn something spanking new every day. Many of the 365 facts learned in the course of a year (or 7,300 facts across the span of time our editor has asked us to report on) are probably useless unless we relate them to principles we have tested and found good and useful.

The distinguished compiler of this book has asked me to sift from all of the many things, big and small, one learns in twenty years of advertising experience and come up with twenty of the most useful. Accordingly, I held a sieve to memory's bin and selected twenty kernels—not enough for a whole loaf, perhaps, but enough to add one man's flavor to this book.

Some of the authors of these chapters have spent fruitful business lifetimes exclusively in one of the three major areas of advertising—those with the advertiser, those with the advertising agency, and those in media. And some, like myself, have spent about half of our time as client and the other half as salesmen or sales managers with important media.

Thus, most of the worthwhile principles that I have learned the hard way are applicable in all branches of advertising—or any other business, for that matter.

This list originally contained some 65 different things which I have learned in 20 years in advertising, ranging from such random notes as "Don't make rash promises" and "Keep a notebook handy for recording ideas" to "Study ways to improve your work flow" and "When a job turns sour, accept responsibility."

However, I was asked to submit twenty and *only* twenty; and yet on contemplative reflection I know I could list 100. Whether the score I have selected are more significant than the possible fourscore I've left out, no one will ever know. But in making the selection I sought to weigh and measure each for the contribution it might make to somebody else's success in this wonderful world called advertising.

1. *Develop Drive.* Advertising is a high-powered, dynamic industry and only the most dynamic men are candidates for the top executive posts. To get there requires initiative, resourcefulness, enthusiasm, energy, call it what you will. I call it *drive.*

   Where do you get drive? Is it something only certain gifted men have—the Henry Kaisers of America who, seemingly by sheer force of will—*drive*—can forge a whole new industry where none existed before, or create a fleet of Liberty ships out of discarded tin cans?

   This ability on the part of the captains of industry to drive ahead with all the organized energy of a locomotive was something that very early in my business career I found lacking in my own gentle personality. I skirmished with tasks at hand rather than boldly and forcefully attacking them. I would dally with and ponder a problem, wondering in envy how men of seemingly boundless energy would tackle the same one.

Reading the profiles of great industrial leaders, time and time again they would be described as men with tremendous drive. And all of a sudden one day I realized that these men were not endowed with certain special natural resources which I did not have. I realized that I had just as much drive as any of them, but the trick they had learned, and which I had to learn, was how to uncork that drive.

The secret of developing drive evolved in a very simple fashion. Reading the life story of R. J. Reynolds on one occasion, I came across a statement by him that helped me to understand the very simplicity of unleashing this force. Asked where he got his tremendous drive, Mr. Reynolds replied, "It isn't drive—it's potato peeling. And the champion potato peeler is the man who peels one potato at a time."

I reflected on this as I thought of the many times at my own desk, harassed by scores, if not hundreds, of details demanding attention, I would evade and rationalize my situation—complaining to my assistants of the tremendous amount of work that had piled up—until I was in a state of lethargy.

The next day I tried Reynolds's champion potato peeling approach and found that I had moved my "mountains of work" in no time at all—and actually felt exhilarated, wanting to wade in and tackle the next problem.

The late James Forrestal, who rose from a sailor boy to be the first Secretary of Defense, was also asked where he got his tremendous amounts of energy and he replied, "I deliberately took on more work than I thought I could accomplish in a given period of time, then forced myself by sheer will-power to do it. It's like cranking up an airplane engine. Turning over by hand an engine is a difficult procedure, but once you have spun the prop, the engine is running and begins to run of its own accord."

Sound simpler[1] Well, it is; and yet it's a lesson which if not learned very early in life may well keep the most talented of advertising men locked in at the lower echelon.

2. *Learn the Technique of the Warm-Up.* Just as Casey Stengel would not put a new pitcher on the mound who had not spent at least twenty minutes in the bull pen warming up, just so you cannot expect to begin working at top efficiency in your job until you have had time to "warm up." The principle is the same in the operation of your car's engine—until it's warmed up, you can't expect peak performance.

Early in my business career I developed the habit of ending each business day by starting a new chore— Part One, perhaps, of a lengthy report which would be that much easier to return to the next morning. Also, I developed the habit of taking the afternoon's mail home with me in the evening—but not to do homework. On the morning train, after a quick glance at the paper, I would read all this correspondence. It helped to wake up—as well as warm up—my business brain. In other words, I had already started before getting to the office; and when I arrived, I was ready to plunge right in.

Each man can develop his own method of "warming up" but there is no doubt in my mind that the principle is one which can be one of life's biggest time savers.

3. *Either You Keep Living Or You Die.* While this may sound very obvious, what I am referring to it this: you must keep your very *self* alive, curious, stimulated, adventurous.

Chiefly, you must keep yourself educated. Read. Have fun. Build things. Go to galleries. Listen to music. Talk. Make jokes. Learn, learn, learn. *Live!* Otherwise, you get soft and stupid. And you find yourself, professionally as well as in every other way, at the bottom of the heap.

Look around when you first enter the world of advertising and you will see that all the men at the top are very vibrantly alive. They are men of many and varied interests. They have a zest for living that seemingly puts them head and shoulders above people in other professions. They are men who are always going places, doing things. They live in a world of imagination and creativity. And each day is an active *new* day, full of living.

4. *Choose Your Work Carefully.* The rule of "love-your-work" is one which completely transcends doing a good job or making money. If you think about it for a moment, you realize that you spend almost two-thirds of your waking hours getting *to* work, getting *through* work, returning *from* work. What you do with these two-thirds can enhance—or destroy—the most important conditions of your life—happiness, peace of mind, personal integrity.

   Certainly there are plenty of examples of men who disliked their life's work but did it outstandingly well. Probably these same men would have been even more successful in another field. Of course, we cannot discount completely aptitude and ability to perform certain types of occupation. But granted these qualifications, the man or woman whose job is his hobby can look forward to a life which is successful in the deepest sense of the word.

5. *Don't Let Security Box You Off.* More good men have been washed up on the shores of the has-beens because they worshipped at the false shrine of security. And what they thought reflected security more often than not turned

out to be a booby-trap that would knock off a Mark V tank.

Most men duck responsibility, for it means sticking their necks out. They prefer the security of a No. 2 or lesser spot where top management won't even know much, or care much, about what they're doing.

Plan to face it—the man who's going places in a career in advertising will have his neck out far and often.

6. *Know* PEOPLE. We have all advised salesmen and, in turn, have been advised, "Know your job and your product." These facts are basic and have been expounded elsewhere in this book. But I would like to explain why knowing people can be of even greater importance. Any man in advertising, particularly one interested in the selling aspects of it, should cultivate the widest possible circle of worthwhile acquaintances. Most people like to help their friends when they can do so without embarrassment or hurt to the companies employing them. A man who knows important people on the right basis never has trouble getting to the right person at the right time, provided he has a logical sales story.

Perhaps no profession does so much business over the luncheon table and at the cocktail bar as advertising—and this is largely because it is a "person-to-person" business. As you develop your circle of acquaintances, you would be wise to index them carefully, even to the point of noting the date on which you last had lunch or a drink—with a tickler as to when you should get together again.

7. *KNOW People.* A corollary to Item 6 above, getting to know people is *knowing* them, understanding them, understanding their motives and aspirations, their feelings, their personal and business hopes and fears.

A good salesman is, first of all, a good practical psychologist. If he can study the man across the desk and get to know him well enough to know "what makes him tick," then he is in a position to influence him favorably. Every conscientious salesman knows his product and keeps his information up to date. But knowing human nature and what motivates people is a somewhat different study.

So in this field, perhaps more than in any other, understanding human motives is of paramount importance if one is to be successful.

8. *Give Yourself Identity.* In advertising you will be meeting hundreds of businessmen—especially if you are in the selling end.

Will they remember you two weeks after you first met them? Probably not unless there is something distinctive about you that makes you more than a name on a calling card.

Let's look into what does make people distinctive and memorable. What's the first thing you think of when you cast up in your mind the image of Marlene Dietrich, Jimmy Durante, F.D.R., Winston Churchill, Brigitte Bardot? Legs, nose, cigarette holder, cigar and, well, the pout.

Each of us has a character tag of sorts; some are affirmative, some negative. What's yours? Is it an affirmative one?

One friend of mine, on an average day, had to see more than twenty-five people. This meant that his appointment calendar had to be run with the efficiency of a one-track railroad line. To impress his steady flow of callers with the importance of being prompt, and not running over their allotted time, he wore *two* wrist watches. *Time* became the personality characteristic by which all came to know him.

9. *Keep Your Eye on The Next Step Up.* This is not intended to say that you should be a job-hopper, although a little of that in the earliest days in an advertising career contributes to what is called "rounding out the man."

I early adopted the philosophy that, just by the sheer progression of time, there had to be new openings at the top and that, by God, one of them was destined for me. When I took my first job as a space representative on a very small magazine, I was determined to learn all the selling tricks in one year—and then move to a larger book, and so on and so on until I was on the staff of the biggest magazine in America. All of which I was able — with luck—to accomplish.

We recently hired a new salesman who had been on the staff of general weekly magazines; and on the day he was hired he revealed to me, "You know, I've been working for years to get this job! I planned five years ago that one day I'd represent *This Week Magazine.*"

In keeping your eye on the next step up, I think it wise to have a long-range objective—the sales manager's job, vice president for marketing, whatever it may be—and then plan your intermediate objectives as stepping stones toward the objective.

10. *Be a Team Player.* When it comes to business, each of us has a lot of the "ham" in him, that alluring quirk which prompts him to want to step forward, stage center, and take the bows and credits for a sale, an idea, a bold new plan that's making money. From the beginning, you must resist the impulse, or you're a ham for life.

If you're a salesman and you bring in 26 pages of business and the president takes you to lunch to express his delight, that's the chance to shine—humbly. You tell him that it was a "team sale"—that the boys in the marketing department, the promotion department, the research department all gave you the tools and ammunition you needed to clinch the business. It makes you look even bigger than you are.

I know of one executive who was slated for bigger and better things—his name was often dropped in board meetings as being a man on the way up. But suddenly it began to go to his head and he became a credit grabber— taking credit for work his associates and subordinates did—and his star lost its lustre overnight. Today the man is sliding down hill fast and it's too late to reverse his field.

11. *Think in Terms of the Other Man's Problems.* Every time you make a call, every time you visit somebody's office, remember that that man has a problem (or he wouldn't have the job). Relate what you have to do with him to his problems. How can you or the services you have to offer directly help him to solve his problem? If you adopt this attitude with every call you make, you can be sure that you'll always be welcomed back another time.

12 *Select a Good Secretary.* There is an old maxim in business that goes, "It is easier to find a new president for the Company than to find a good secretary." And believe me, it's true.

In your absence from the office, your secretary is you; and how she performs, how her personality is projected, all reflects on you.

Confide in your secretary; keep nothing from her. "Office Wife" is no misnomer if you and your secretary are a working team. An efficient, pleasant secretary can be the greatest asset a man can have in developing a successful business career.

13. *Be a Fact Man.* The advertising profession has its share of hole-in-the-head oratory. But it seldom pays off. Early establish a reputation for yourself as being a straightforward, hard-facts fellow who only opens his mouth when he has something important to say.

14. *Learn the Technical Side.* And here I don't mean "Madison Avenueese," but the hard-core language that shows you know your business, as indeed you must. Know the various kinds of printing processes—letter press, offset, gravure, etc.—about engravings and "progs," about photography and Type-C prints, about art and copy, mechanicals and layouts. Learning the language isn't enough; you have to know the various techniques.

15. *Take Your Vacations!* One thing that Management will never thank you for is passing up your vacation to keep on the job. And anybody worth his salt works too doggone hard not to get away from the shop when he has the opportunity to forget and relax.

16. *Practice Creativity.* I once asked a very brilliant agency copywriter how he attained his degree of creativity and he astounded me by answering, "Practice." He went on to explain that the creative process is something that can be learned (but not necessarily taught) and that practice at the subject made one more and more proficient. Regardless of the phase of advertising you adopt in your career, the greater measure of creative effort you can bring to it, the more successful you will be.

17. *Develop Personal Public Relations.* Giant companies will pay millions of dollars to public relations men to tell them how to offer their best face to the world. The

conscientious advertising man will read several of the many good books on this subject to acquaint himself with the principles of public relations and then relate them to his own career.

18. Be *Optimistic and Open-Minded.* Sounds silly, I suppose, but in my twenty years of advertising I've crossed paths with pessimism and close-mindedness more often than I have the opposite.

For example, a major manufacturing company wanted a "spectacular" in print and approached three magazines with their idea for a 32-page insert. Sales representatives for the first two magazines merely shook their heads and said, "Presents a mechanical problem we can't handle."

But the salesman for *The Readers Digest* said, "Let me try and work out the details with our production department."

He was optimistic and open-minded. He got the order for 30 pages at more than $30,000 a page!

19. *Strategies and Tactics.* These primarily military terms rarely are adopted by the advertising man until he is well along in life and his career. But adoption of the principles of strategy and tactics by the young aspiring advertising executive will help him to organize and develop better campaigns, product or media sales, and help him to fit his own ambitions into a pattern that will enable him to measure the progress of his career growth.

20. *Keep Your Nose Clean.* Once in a while a dirty-nosed fellow does very well, indeed, in this business. But for the most part, he is locked in at the lower echelons because he was found out early in his career.

Chester H. Lang

Graduated A.B. from University of Michigan, Honorary LL.D. degrees from Michigan and Union College. During 36 years with General Electric Co. he served as Comptroller of the Budget, Manager of Advertising and Sales Promotion, Manager of Apparatus Sales, Chairman of G. E. War Projects Committee. Charge of Public Relations and Educational Relations. Vice President in 1941 until retirement in 1955.

No Tight Little Island

Chester H. Lang

In putting down the precepts that guided me in my advertising career, I am actually expressing attitudes that I absorbed from people who had been with the General Electric Company since it was born—and most of these people were not in advertising. In General Electric, advertising has never been a tight little island sitting off somewhere on the fringe of the business. Every function and every person in the business has always been market-oriented—not only towards today's markets, but also towards the markets of the future.

1. I suppose Mr. Edison had a lot to do with market-conditioning his contemporaries and his heirs in the General Electric Company. Starting with a light bulb in 1879, he and his associates set about inventing a complete electric generating and distribution system to make the light bulb a marketable product. Shortly thereafter, another device for utilizing electric power appeared, a practical motor, and the electrical industry started out on a dizzying growth curve that has kept all of us in it excited throughout our business careers.

2. General Electric's advertising, from the start, has been informed, inspired, and directed by excitement and belief—belief in new markets, new products, new heights for the American economy. But people in advertising merely reflected a sense of adventure that permeated all kinds of work in all the companies that had a hand in creating a new America.

3. Some of the more speculative phrases and promises that our advertising men put into the minds of the American people constituted promises on which our engineers and scientists had to make good. Conversely one of the greatest engineers and mathematicians this country has ever known, the beloved Charles Proteus Steinmetz, proved himself to be a real "idea man" in advertising. Shortly after the First World War, a young publicity man asked Steinmetz's help in making electrical equipment vivid and appealing to the average newspaper reader. After a couple of thoughtful puffs on his famous cigar, the mathematical wizard offered this formula:

   "One horsepower equals the muscle work of about twenty-two men—big men." And he continued, "There are machines coming out of General Electric which can do more work than the entire slave population of this country at the time of the Civil War." Steinmetz then asked if this would interest the average reader. It certainly did. Many advertising and promotional series were based on the image that Steinmetz furnished.

4. In any company pervaded by an exciting sense of mission, everybody is an advertising man because everybody is a marketing man. However, just as madness has its method, excitement and a sense of mission must have some pattern and substance. It can't be all fritter, froth, and patter.

5. I have often been asked if I believe in any *formula* for effective advertising. Well, in a sense, I do. If I were asked to give a formula for long-range effectiveness in advertising, I would give these three points:

    a. Identify your markets, both actual and potential.

    b. Use every available tool of communication, of course, but beyond that, look for ingenious innovations, even small ones.

    c. Finally, I'd say, stick with it.

In my own company, this business of proper market identification can be traced right back to Edison. After World War I, when Mr. Swope became President of the General Electric Company, he made a decision which had a healthful effect not only on the direction of the General Electric Company, but also on the nature of the Company's advertising. General Electric embarked on a long range and continuing campaign to create a consciousness of *electrical living* in the mind of the American consumer. This decision was taken at a time when only lamps and a few small appliances manufactured by the Company brought the "Initials of a Friend," as the General Electric Monogram was known in those days, into the American home.

6. The Electric Living campaign—which has really never stopped —worked for the Company's natural sales allies—the electric utilities—with ads pointing out how electricity, despite its ever increasing usefulness, was held to a low cost in a generally rising market. Washing machine manufacturers who used motors and other components made by General Electric also found us speaking to their customers, telling them how, for one

penny, electricity would drive their washing machines for twenty minutes. We didn't sell washing machines then, but we sold component motors; and we didn't sell electricity, but we sold turbine-generators. With one theme, "Electrical Living," we obtained recognition for the Monogram in many markets. And the theme still has validity and vitality. Our ads in the '20's called electricity "the biggest penny's worth in history." Thirty years later we could still put out industry ads featuring "electricity—today's greatest bargain."

7. The goal of all advertising should be to sell products, but that doesn't mean it cannot and should not have scope, breadth, and inspiration. One of my favorite campaigns in the late 20's was the "Any Woman" series. It had heads like this: "Any woman who does anything which a little motor can do is working for 3 cents an hour!" I think ads like that made the point. The forceful and imaginative presentation of truth in this case is a variant of the formula that Steinmetz furnished.

8. An entire business, then, not just its advertising function, should pick the right markets early in the game. This sounds obvious, I know. I also know that a lot of companies that were around when I came to the General Electric Company are not around today. In my opinion, one of the big reasons why they are not among the survivors is that their early decisions on choice of markets contained the seeds of their demise instead of their future growth.

9. And if you pick the right market, how do you talk to it? One of the uneasy questions that advertisers are supposed to be asking themselves about the market is, "Is Anybody Listening?" A much more fundamental concern, in my opinion, should be, "Am I listening?" I mean *listening*

to the market! Thirty-five years ago, my company had a market research component in advertising. This component was charged with listening to the market, continuously and formally. We had always done this in an informal way. Today, such a component may be found in each of our sales organizations. Marketing people in General Electric tell me today that there is far more work to be done in learning to listen intelligently to the market than there is in trying to measure impact and readership, however valuable these studies may be.

10. When you have identified both actual and potential markets, it may be smart to figure out the most *economical* way of talking to your customers. In all respects, the most effective and economical strategy I know for doing this is to establish, broadly and symbolically, an image of your company and then to carry this single image into all of your markets. This is not "in lieu of" product promotion; *it is product -promotion.* In General Electric (the only company from which I can authoritatively take my examples), we ambitiously saw the farms, the homes, and the industries of America as our markets long before we had made significant penetrations of all of them. Our one message to all of these markets turned on the benefits of electricity—electrical farming, electrical living, electrical producing. The image we wanted to have associated with this electrical consciousness was the General Electric Monogram.

11. Any good Company is more than the sum of its products. For this reason, a deliberate decision was made in the 20's to establish the Monogram as widely as possible as General Elec-tric's symbol of quality. Although it didn't happen overnight, a number of other symbols used by the Company—all of which had acquired great prestige in limited areas—were discarded one after the

other. I'm talking about names like Mazda, Edison, Telechron, and others. We wanted to register with our customers as General Electric. And then we wanted to diversify and multiply our electrical products to justify both parts of this name, the *General* as well as the *Electric.* The products didn't necessarily come first. Our early advertising included certain products —notably major appliances—that we didn't even make at the time! This, I think, was unique. Clearly, then, we believed that advertising should be inspired in part by some internal image of the company's natural direction and future markets, not just by the products made at the time.

12. Like other companies, General Electric has had a series of slogans, some better than others in presenting an image of the company to its markets. What interests me is that it seems to take years to develop an accurate concept of what the company really represents so that it can be adequately described in its slogan We've had all these slogans:

"The Initials of a Friend."

"More Goods for More People at Less Cost."

"You Can Put Your Confidence in General Electric."

All of them had their value in their time. But it really took a backward look at what we had been doing over the years—and the stimulus of the great growth period that followed World War II—for us to be able to realize and to say without fear of contradiction that "Progress Is Our Most Important Product."

13. Now for the second point in my "formula" for effective advertising. Let me elaborate on what I meant when I said that an advertising man should use every available tool of communication and, beyond that, should search out new tools. Taking my examples again from the

General Electric Company, I can say that some of us in our exuberance have really stretched for novelty, but not really for novelty's sake alone.

Back in 1932, for example, we were looking for a novel way to start up the new 50,000-watt transmitter for radio station WGY. Through the cooperation of the Navy, I had the exciting experience of taking a 24-hour roundtrip ride from Lakehurst to Schenectady, in the U.S. Dirigible *Los Angeles.* My mission over Schenectady was to blow a police whistle that would start up the transmitter on the ground by sending a signal along a beam of light. I must say that the crew aboard the *Los Angeles* remained skeptical until they received a message of congratulations from their buddies aboard the *Akron,* which was then maneuvering with the Pacific fleet off California! They had heard the program as carried direct by NBC's national network. The beam-of-light trick was a novelty at the time, but it has since been seen by several million people during "House of Magic" presentations. This was a publicity stunt, of course, but it also had great and genuine value in dramatizing the still young radio industry.

14. General Electric's alertness to new means of communication had something to do with the fact that we had had a hand in developing several of them—radio, TV, and motion pictures.

WGY broadcast its first test concert in 1922. Just a few years after that, when we were running out of amateur singers and musicians in Schenectady, we concocted a telegraphic wire network, running south to New York City and west to Cleveland, for the selfish purpose of tapping a far larger supply of talent to provide programs for the radios we hoped to sell.

Then, in 1928, we broadcast our first TV drama.

15. Most people think of the business motion picture as an off shoot of the entertainment film. The fact is that some of the first films to come out of Edison's laboratory in 1888 were produced for advertising purposes! In 1909, General Electric established itself as a pioneer in the industrial-sponsored film field with a picture promoting the sale of appliances. It was produced for the Company by Essanay in Chicago and the title was "Every Husband's Opportunity." Our own motion picture production went into action in 1912, its first "epic" being a film record of the electrification of the Butte, Anaconda, and Pacific Railroad line.

I wish people could see our first farm "flicker," which was made in 1913 at a cost of $985. The shooting location was on the properties of the Pacific Gas and Electric Company and the story was about a boy who left the farm for a "better life," but returned when his father electrified the farm and offered him comforts and work-saving devices that would have created envy in the big town. The story made us weep once because we were young and naive; if we didn't laugh today, it might make us weep because we are older and nostalgic. So we have used motion pictures both early and late.

16. One of the most comprehensive, imaginative, and novel market development schemes ever devised in the General Electric Company was "More Power to America." The objectives of More Power to America were to promote the benefits of electricity to our industry, farm and community markets, utilizing every promotional tool known or conceivable, and enlisting the support of the nation's electrical utilities. Promotional media included industry publications, space advertising, productivity forums, film programs, and special exhibits. One special exhibit—to give you an idea of what we mean here—

was a sleek, 10-car train, the More Power to America Special, a visual summation of General Electric's contributions in the field of electrical apparatus to the progress of industrial America. Collected within the space of ten railroad cars were more than 2,000 electrical products, processes, and techniques. They ranged from delicate aircraft instruments to models of gigantic steel mill control equipment. Starting out on April 18, 1950, the train began a year-long jaunt across the nation, bringing an overwhelming story of progress to invitation audiences in 150 cities of the United States.

17. I've seen many gimmicks in my time. If I had to generalize I'd say that the more incredible and impossible they seemed at first brush, the more they paid off in the end. I've bought some wild and beautiful ideas in my day. I've probably squelched some equally good ones, too. That's the sad thing in this business. If inadvertently you kill a man's brain children, you may kill the man too as a creating and contributing individual. And no one will ever be the wiser—not even your victim. I guess I can't help slipping this caution in here for the mature men in this advertising business rather than for the younger people: Try to develop someone—maybe even your wife—who'll kick you in the pants when you get too smug about your own ability to pick a winner. It's a real danger, believe me.

18. Perhaps I'd better come to that third and final point. If you've done a good job of picking your market, and if you've shown creativity in using and developing your tools of communication, what remains to be done? Why, sticking to it, of course! To recall again that tantalizing question, "Is anybody listening?" I would again approach it from a different point of view and say, "Are you still listening?" Are you talking continuously

and persistently enough to know that you have not lost your market by default? In the more direct and measurable method of communication represented by public speaking, my experience led me to conclude that no audience loses interest until the speaker loses interest—and conviction and enthusiasm.

19. In advertising, one of the best measures of your interest and belief that the customer can go by is your continuity of communication with him. In advertising, intermittent communication is no communication. You've got to keep at it. This decision may depend more on your boss than on you—but not entirely. Even without budget restrictions, some advertising men *flirt* with different customer groups instead of entering into sober, honorable, and continuing relationships with them. This is fatal. When I look back on advertising in General Electric, I am struck by the fact that many of our themes, campaigns and markets are the same as they were thirty to forty years ago.

To show you what I mean, the "Electrical Living" campaign of 35 years ago has become today's "Live Better Electrically" (actually an industry-wide campaign supported by General Electric among others.) The old "Home of a Hundred Comforts" has become today's "Medallion Home." The theme that we used when the automobile (and I) were young, "Light Is the Best Policeman," is now "Light Up and Live." Even the "More Power to America" train was, in a sense, an updated million-dollar version of a horse-drawn apparatus float which the Thompson-Houston Electric Company— one of the companies whose merger formed General Electric—placed in a Fourth of July parade of 1890 to exhibit the progress of the electrical industry. Products and conditions have evolved, yet General Electric is still using some old themes with some old and abiding markets. This could mean that we hadn't developed as we should have; however, I'm sure it really means that our early pinpointing of markets was essentially correct and that our themes were comprehensive enough and far-sighted enough to be valid even today.

20. One last point. Every generation of advertising men seems to be *put in the 'position of defending itself.* Or maybe some of us develop a defensive outlook to start with. In any event, new weapons are being continuously devised to carry the battle of self-justification to an enemy who may not always exist. I've spent a lot of time on both sides of the desk, as an advertising manager and as a sales and marketing manager. Current methods of "measuring" advertising are of great value. But given their degree of development, I think that enlightened management will have to be satisfied with determining that the objectives of advertising correspond with the objective of the business. In looking back, I know I cannot prove that today's widespread "electrical living" measures the success of all the advertising that General Electric directed to the home, the farm, and the factory over many, many decades. I can't prove it, yet as far as I'm concerned, the cause-and effect relationship is as obvious as the fact that Christianity in Pogoland followed the landing of missionaries and did not develop as an evolutionary result of voodoo. Apparently I had—and have—faith in the worth and power of my old calling. Have some yourself!

N. J. Leigh

Into the world, 1902, into business 1915 with faked working papers. First job-errand boy Blackman Ross, advertising agency, predecessor to Compton Advertising, Inc. After four-year apprenticeship, joined J. R. Mayers Co., display brokers, as sales assistant.

In 1921 moved to Einson-Freeman Co. as salesman. Elected Vice President 1928. In 1935 organized a group that bought business from M. M. Einson and was chosen President. Served for 16 years and was elected Chairman of Board of Directors, 1951.

On Working Efficiency and Other Pointers

1. TALKING BEFORE GROUPS

Make the mechanics of the talk work smoothly. Drill the helpers. If one blunders, have a stock phrase or an alternate exhibit to use. And above all, have a "storm shelter" which may be an amusing story about the industry as a whole or a quickie about advertising to slip in if there is a real mix-up. Remember, the audience never knows your sequence or discomfort.

Laughs

Blunders on the platform sometimes strike an audience as funny. Comedians work days for a single laugh and if you hit one accidentally consider it a "jack pot" and build on it ... fast. Example, telling the story of the Rheingold contest I made a slip about the boys at the bars doing some multiple voting which brought a big laugh. I covered with a reference to the boys making book on the contest winner, which brought a second laugh.

Cartoon stories

The best kind of a platform quickie is to describe a cartoon and give the gag line under it. Example, the Rheingold contest cartoon in the *New Yorker* showing two men at a bar in an argument. One points to the Rheingold contest posters back of the bar and says, "You see, Eddie, in Russia they'd appoint a Miss Rhein-gold."

2. PERSONAL SELLING

Selling is communication. First, have something to get over ... a must. Then use every means you can think of to put it over. Phone, letter, wire, secretary, cartoon reference—anything. People (and all buyers are people) are indifferent, preoccupied, oblivious of your needs and to get an idea across calls for a breakthrough. The greatest obstacle in selling is lack of communication . . . the greatest help is knowing how to communicate to a specific buyer.

Readers and non-readers

Ever notice that some people read all letters and some never seem to remember a letter or memorandum . . . usually because they never read it.

We had an art director, a notorious type of non-reader, who had a habit of putting all memos on his wall with a push tack. Somehow he felt if he left them there, the contents would seep into his brain. It never happened but he would always counter your annoyance with, "See, I've got it right here," and point to the memo on the wall.

Some buyers are like that and the first thing to find out about a man is how to find your way into his brain.

Handicapped people

Practically every person has in his family or intimate circle the concern of working with someone who is physically handicapped.

Much has been written advising young salesmen to find out buyers' hobbies . . . golf, swimming or gardening, and then talking to them about those matters.

I have found almost invariably that if you can reach the matter of helping a handicapped person in whom the other man is interested, you can reach him far more effectively and intimately through interest and possibly through suggestions on his particular problem with a handicapped person.

3. ADMINISTRATION

Administration is mostly listening . . . and, of course, asking questions. Curious, how most important decisions in a company's operations will solve themselves if someone in authority will take the time and have the patience to listen attentively to the people involved, collect all the facts and suggestions that are offered.

A good communicator is often a poor listener . . . and usually the wrong man for inside administration. He must discipline himself to listen and as his controls to induce patience become strained, he becomes more and more uncomfortable. But it's often the price we must pay for a thoughtful and right decision.

4. SALES INSPIRATION

The greatest source of inspiration for salesmen is enthusiasm for a product or for an idea. Can it be generated on order?

Yes! How? By first assembling all the "reasons why" and then having imaginative people interpret the facts before men in a group . . . not individually.

Enthusiasm is contagious. It will grow rapidly from man to man and finally infect even the most skeptical treasurer. But it must be planned and the talk infused with a restless desire to get out and do it by the man who is making it.

5. INVESTMENTS

The greatest lesson I have learned about handling money is not to jump around. It takes a lifetime to learn and know a business and equally long to learn one field of investing capital.

Even in the study of securities there is a distinct specialization by the "pros" and surely no amateur can take the time to even read half of the good literature available in any restricted field of securities, such as natural gas or insurance companies or supermarket chains.

How then can any business man expect to call the shots in real estate or radio stations or bowling alleys which now seem to be a challenge to guess the future? Except for a lucky shot, money is made by people who think hard and study and worry and fret before they make a commitment.

6. CONFIDENCE

Advisers are swell. Lawyers, accountants, tax experts, engineers, all earn their money. It pays to listen. But remember, a man must make a decision and he must finally rely on his own judgment. What is confidence?

Mostly it's half looking backward on experience and half a gamble on the future. Now, the retrospective part is analyzing every major decision of the past for good or bad, with a long look inside one's consciousness. The gamble is to what extent can I afford to make a mistake.

Confidence should be based on soul searching.

7. ADVISORS

One great value in asking for or in buying advice is a reference to sources. So many bold projects that sound original and imaginative have been tried or done before. Usually the specialist, a tax advisor, an engineer, or a financial lawyer all know and can pinpoint sources for past experience in the project at hand.

The question to ask is: has it ever been done before? Where and how? Let's not start where they started, but build on their base, learn about their mistakes.

8. SOCIAL ROOTS

Friendships make society but social roots are more than that. They are the projection of the family outward into the community . . . the tentacles of contact through children, the church plan and other interests that go far deeper.

In the shifting of men and families from city to city so often necessary in large corporations, the emphasis in handling the individual should be on his special social roots and where and how they can be re-grafted in the new community. Too often the matter is dismissed with, "Oh, you'll get to know people quickly in Cincinnati." That's not enough.

9. WHERE YOU LIVE

People say, "Oh, if I could only live in California . . . Florida or the Virgin Islands, I would be much happier." They fail to realize that they take their problems with them right inside the little old bean.

For most people a geographical escape is just an illusion. It doesn't make much difference where you live. What counts is the satisfaction of the individual: the thrills and disappointment of his job, the fun of his pleasure time or the quiet contemplation of his family's future.

These things do not depend on a place or climate but a grasp of the realities of life and a kindly adjustment to them.

10. BOREDOM

Insurance people and advisors all say, "Develop a hobby for your retirement years." But they seldom show the other side of the coin which is that having nothing to do is a crushing bore!

Nursery school teachers describe some of the things with which they interest children as "busy work." Now for any thoughtful adult, "busy work" for the sake of itself is pretty silly, but it is a fact that the tough jobs of business are not really appreciated by any but the retired or the idle.

In fact, it always seemed desirable to have more things to do than there are hours in the day. Real wealth to me is the luxury of choice—which job to take on.

11. TRAVEL

Movement from place to place . . . even if you've been there before is stimulating and if the trip is to a new part of the country it is especially exciting. We all need this occasional shot in the arm and photographs help us re-live the trip for years to come.

But our text for today is not to let the petty annoyances of travel interfere with the larger purpose and value of the trip. Too many people do just that.

Bags get lost. Laundry does not come back on time. Once in a while an airplane reservation clerk is venal and will sell out your space for a $20 tip. But it's all a part of the business of travel and if it bothers you too much, you're better off at home.

12. RELAXATION

As a normally intense person I am constantly urged by my well-meaning family and friends to relax . . . take it easy . . . don't press so hard or you'll kill yourself.

Well, what makes you think I want to relax? Or that it is necessary for me? Or that I enjoy being relaxed more than being tensed up?

Tensions are a part of living. The sale of tranquilizer drugs which people seem to be eating like popcorn indicates that most people want to avoid tensions. But they are one force in life that gets things done. I hate to think of all the lazy slipshod jobs and thinking that can be attributed to the Miltown phobia . . . the desire to avoid tensions.

13. SLEEP

Sleep is a tool of living, a necessary part of every 24-hour span, but it should not be a necessity at routine intervals or the lack of it permitted to be a source of worry.

The high sale of sleeping pills indicates a large part of the population must feel a need for sleep that exists in the mind but that is not demanded by the body. The Mellon Institute for Industrial Research of the University of Pittsburgh did a study on sleep in the early 1930's that determined my attitude toward sleep for a whole lifetime.

In brief, that study concluded that if left alone the body and mind would demand and get the sleep it needed. The need for sleep varies greatly with the individual. Just wait till you're sleepy and then sleep. It's that simple.

14. DIET CONTROLS

Habits mechanize a large part of living. They are the automation of life. Good or bad, they control our destiny to a far greater degree than we realize.

This is especially true in the matter of weight control where we should not make decisions at every mealtime. They must be grooved into a routine habit. Once this is accomplished, weight control is easy.

It's not the occasional splurge at a party that adds weight but the day in and day out habits of eating. A recent magazine article was headed, "Crash diets are the bunk," but it should have added in equally large type, "Crash habits do the job."

15. TEACHING

The best teachers are the best listeners. It takes a special kind of person to be a good teacher. They're rare and always command my respect.

Because teaching involves the subordination of the teacher to the student . . . the trainer to the animal . . . the leader to a follower, not many people have the gift of teaching; a projection of self into others that takes patience, control and above all a satisfaction with the accomplishment inherent in the teaching process. Good teachers have a dedication to others that is one of the most inspiring aspects of our society. We should respect it.

16. DRINKING

My only thought about this important aspect of living today is "if you're on, don't drink." But use "on" in the theatrical sense of "on stage" and it includes all kinds of business or other meetings where you are expected to perform.

There is just too much competition in business to take a chance on being five or ten per cent less bright than you might be without the dulling and depressive effects of alcohol. Barnum once said that Jumbo was the biggest elephant in the world by only one inch; often it's that little bit of extra sharp judgment that may influence your whole business life.

17. WORKING EFFICIENCY

Some people start the day with a bang and do their best work in the early morning. Others start the day slowly and reach their peak of ability at the late afternoon or evening.

It's important to recognize when and how you do your best work and then cater to that tendency. Fatigue is probably responsible for more bad decisions than any other one cause. If possible, postpone or delay decisions and meetings until you feel like handling them. Watch the time of the day and conditions when you feel right.

And that's not the day of a hangover.

18. COMPLAINTS

Face up to it. If your company has fallen down on delivery or made a mistake, don't avoid the irate customer. See him promptly and let him take it all out on you. Be the whipping boy for your company.

More irritation has been compounded from a little pimple to a sore boil by neglect and by avoiding a meeting than for any other reason.

The injured party is seldom as badly off as he thinks he is and will often dramatize his misfortune at your expense. Let him put on the show and be the humble suppliant victim. It's the only way to get it behind you.

19. NEW PEOPLE

Every new human contact is an exciting challenge if you approach it in the right way. Every person has an "island within" which will usually be revealed if you are gracious and willing to listen. Every good business contact is an opportunity for advancement if you handle it well.

It pays to develop an ingratiating "first front." Whether you can hold a person's interest or even want to do so is aside from the point here. The object is to suggest a study of the first five or ten minutes of how you handle a first meeting. The slight smile, the courteous reference, the polite questions are all important.

20. CONVERSATION

Ever think in advance of what you will bring to a party in the way of ideas to interest the people there?

The best conversations are "bull sessions" in which there is a relaxed atmosphere and a subject of mutual interest. But often the subject must be planted—introduced at the right time.

My most enjoyable conversations have been with people who are articulate and willing to talk about their own work . . . the editor of a steel trade paper who discussed steel mills later took me through one because my interest had been generated in our conversations ... a psychiatrist who talked about his medical specialty ... a money man who discussed the evaluation of capital risks in various areas.

Conversation can be fun.

J. Gordon Lippincott

Graduate of Swarthmore and Columbia. Taught at Pratt Institute and was for many years associated with the late Donald Dohner, pioneer industrial designer. Author of *Design For Business* published in 1947. Co-founder of Lippincott and Margulies in 1946. Since its inception this company has tackled more than 1500 design projects. It was a pioneer in using graphic elements as a marketing tool in integrated relationship to advertising, sales promotion, point-of-purchase, etc.

Twenty Things About Packaging We Have Learned in Twenty Years

J Gordon Lippincott

Packaging

The pace of package development has been so rapid that most of the twenty things we have learned here at Lippincott & Margulies have been developed in the recent years. Sometimes, however, in the pace of current innovation, we forget some of the fundamentals that we learned many years ago. Let's think about some of these packaging fundamentals first.

1. "A PACKAGE SHOULD LOOK LIKE WHAT IT IS"

This sounds like an obvious statement, but it is surprising how many times it is forgotten. For example, if you are packaging beer, don't dress it up so much that it looks like champagne or a vintage wine. Consumers in today's crowded shopping markets have preconceived mental images of what a product looks like. If you put your product in a package that people do not identify "in a flash" with the product they have in mind, you will lose sales. It would be most difficult, for example, to market a ketchup in a glass jar of peanut butter proportions, because it would take a lot of explaining to people that "this is ketchup."

2. "EVERY PACKAGE MUST OFFER A BELIEVABLE CONSUMER BENEFIT"

In packaged merchandise, nobody wants to sell a commodity where only price influences the buy-decision. A believable consumer benefit is not easy to find in many product lines. But good creative innovation can develop believable consumer benefits (real or imagined) and many successful packages and marketing campaigns have been built around this fundamental principle. The Tareyton Dual Filter cigarette, with the believable advantages of two kinds of filters in a single cigarette and with a package that expresses this duality, is a successful example of this fundamental rule. It is getting harder and harder to make a profit with a "me-too" product.

3. "YOUR PACKAGES AND YOUR ADS SHOULD SPEAK THE SAME VISUAL LANGUAGE"

I am reminded of a recent ad in *Life* for chocolate-covered cherries. The photograph was luscious—you could almost smell the chocolate as it poured out of a ladle onto a ripe, juicy cherry-color photography at its best! But did the package speak the same visual language? No! The package illustrated a rubbery-looking chocolate with a synthetic red cherry in an overall format that was most unexciting, let alone having any visual taste appeal. The purpose of the advertising was, through very effective taste appeal, to spark the desire to buy, but if the consumer seeing the package at the point-of-sale has no "flash-back" to the ad impulse, much of the ad investment is lost.

4. "A PACKAGE MUST BE VIEWED IN ITS MARKETING CONTEXT"

It is simply not possible or realistic to evaluate a package per se on an executive desk. For example, we were measuring the visibility of a proposed new package vs. the present package of a well-known, nationally advertised brand. Intuitively, we knew the new package had greater legibility. The letter forms were cleaner, there was more "air" in the layout. Any competent artist would agree that the new design had greater legibility.

The two packages were exposed to consumers in a tachisto-scope test—that is, respondents were shown a colored slide film of the proposed new package and the old package on a supermarket shelf along with other packages. The first exposure was a flash of 1/100th of a second, and successive exposures were for longer duration until the respondents could identify all the packages in the picture. The interesting point here is that the respondents identified the old package faster, even though the newer proposed package was "more legible." Why did they identify the old package first? They identified it first *because they were familiar with it,* through years of heavy advertising and product use. For us to evaluate the effectiveness of the new package without considering the total market implications of advertising and use would be unrealistic. For management to say the old package is better because people see it quicker is also unrealistic. They would see the new package even faster once it became well-known.

5. "CONSIDER A 'GREAT CORPORATE NAME' AS THE ENDORSEMENT FOR NEW BRANDS"

For a good many years, the "Procter & Gamble approach" has been considered the ideal way to launch new products: i.e., a separate advertising budget, a separate brand manager, and a great big push—and no one can deny that P & G have been immensely successful. However, it is interesting to note that even P & G are now putting a corporate endorsement on new brands. The realistic facts are that it costs so much to launch a new product today that few companies have the promotional dollars left to market a completely unrelated line of items. More and more companies such as Johnson's Wax, for example, are recognizing the advantage of *building a favorable corporate image and effectively exploiting this on the package,* using words such as "By the makers of Johnson's Wax." This has sparked, in recent years, a strong trend toward corporate identity programs where a system of communications is established which tells the public the filial relationship between the parent corporation, its divisions and its brands. Corporations are increasingly interested in building a favorable corporate image so that this endorsement applied to new products can increase consumer acceptance. Some companies have carried this so far as to practically eliminate all brand names. For example, when General Electric bought Telechron they acquired a respected and well-known brand name. However, as a matter of policy, the name Telechron was dropped in favor of building a single great corporate name.

General Foods, with its many divisions and dozens of nationally advertised brands, is finding it desirable to advertise "Tested and Approved by General Foods Kitchens," with a new corporate trademark. This is appearing also on more and more of their packaging. Why this trend? Because there are simply too many new brands for the consumer to remember and the endorsement of a well-known and accepted corporation is needed today for more effective marketing.

6. "PEOPLE HAVE LIMITED BRAND VOCABULARIES"

Perhaps you never stopped to think about it, but the human mind seems to have a limited number of brand names that it can effectively remember and recall. We did some probing on this subject a good many years ago and found the following:

a. The word vocabulary of the average American is approximately 5000, of which considerably fewer than 3000 are used in everyday life.

b. The brand name vocabulary (names such as Buick, Coca-Cola, Electrolux, etc.) is 1180 names.

Apparently, when the consumer learns a new brand name, he forgets some of the older brand names he was formerly familiar with. The important concept here is that the consumer appears to have a *limited* brand vocabulary and getting your brand name in the "memory bank" of the average person is an increasingly costly and difficult job.

The Registrar of Copyright, the Library of Congress, in Washington, D.C., tells us that there are an average of 15,000 new brand names applied for each year, and that there are approximately 300,000 active brand names in America today. Small wonder then that our communications channels are overcrowded! What does all this mean to effective packaging? It means that your package should be very carefully designed, that it should be simple, that it should not be changed too often, and that it should be effectively coordinated with advertising and all other forms of promotion in order to achieve maximum penetration.

7. "KEEP ALERT TO PACKAGING INNOVATIONS"

We seem to live in an age of "new and improved." There was a time when simply putting a yellow patch saying "New" on a package was enough to increase sales. The consumer today is, of course, far more sophisticated, and to build a genuine increment of growth requires a lot more than the mere claim of newness or a gimmick. There is no doubt, however, that true innovation—a believable improved consumer benefit—does command consumer attention and increase sales. Innovation is rarely "something you bump into." It is more likely to be continuous research and patient searching of many ideas to distill the few good ones. A great deal of packaging innovation comes from packaging suppliers. Amazingly, many corporations close their channels of communications with these suppliers because package innovation is reviewed by purchasing departments who think primarily in terms of cost. It is almost axiomatic that every new convenience package costs more—the squeeze bottle costs more than glass; the aerosol can cost more than the squeeze bottle. Milk in a carton costs more than milk in returnable bottles, but each of these packages, when first introduced, offered the consumer a demonstrable benefit for which she was *willing to pay more.* The lowest price is no longer the dominant criterion in imaginative package planning today. The real criterion is "Are we offering the consumer something better at a price she is willing to pay?"

8. "TAKE IT EASY ON WHEELING AND DEALING"

For some reason, most inexperienced brand managers feel that the fastest way to increase sales is to reduce price or give something away. It is true that these actions will increase sales but, after all, is this the corporate goal? It seems to me most stockholders would rather see the brand manager increase profits. It has been my experience that increasing profits requires a far more skillful marketing effort than the rather obvious and unimaginative practice of wheeling and dealing. Good creative planning can find other ways of increasing sales. *The great danger of too many deals is that it lowers the value of the 'product in the consumer's mind and, if done too often, the deal ceases to he an incentive.* In many highly competitive fields such as breakfast cereals where deals of one sort or another appear most of the time, the whole value of the deal as a sales stimulus is questionable.

It is highly probable that wheeling and dealing hurts the brand image, lessens the impact of the package on the shelf by making it busier and ends up with some disappointment in the consumer's mind because so many deals fail in giving the consumer sustained and genuine value. What is better than deals? Continued improvement and innovation—a better product in a better package, with more effective point-of-sale displays. Within this concept you can still have a deal or special promotion once or twice a year and then it would be believable. Some companies have been highly successful without ever cutting price—Gillette in safety razors, for example.

9. "CONSIDER THE STORE OPERATOR IN PACKAGE PLANNING"

Whether a product is accepted or not by a supermarket chain is increasingly the crucial sales hurdle for a marketer of packaged merchandise today. Obviously, it is increasingly difficult to get supermarket operators to stock "me-too" items. If he has six instant coffees, why should he take a seventh? If he has three kinds of toilet tissue, why stock a fourth? And so on. Getting to the point-of-sale at all, then, is becoming an increasingly difficult task and one that is best solved by appealing to the supermarket operator's own self-interest. Many manufacturers have taken just the opposite attack—they have brought out added sizes and flavors to gain more shelf facings.

This, of course, is wonderful if you can get away with it, but so many companies are doing it that it is beginning to backfire. A sound creative approach is to study the supermarket operator's problems, particularly from the point of view of the stock clerk. A major cost of the supermarket operator is in the area of "housekeeping." Designing packages that are easier to mark and identify—designing more effective merchandisers and clearly demonstrating to the supermarket buyer that in sales tests your packages are effective profit makers—these are typical potent persuaders.

10. "REVIEW PACKAGE EFFECTIVENESS EACH YEAR"

One of the most important questions facing marketers today is to know when to change a package. Obviously, a package should not be changed just for the sake of change. Some packages are mighty effective marketing tools just as they are—the Lucky Strike cigarette package, for example. Others require almost continuous upgrading as new techniques are discovered —cake mixes, for example, where taste appeal in illustration is so important. It is important to remember that the competitive environment of a given brand is not static. A package which is effective one year may be slightly obsolete the next and completely obsolete five years later because of advances by competitive brands. A careful yearly review of every package is very much in order for every marketer of nationally advertised brands. Usually such a review is keyed with overall marketing plans so that the package can be evaluated in context with the marketing situation. All this goes a long way toward preventing a loss in share of markets by a more aggressive competitor.

11. "RESEARCH EVERY SIGNIFICANT PROPOSED PACKAGE CHANGE"

In the early days of the aviation industry, the good pilots were those who were "good in flying by the seat of their pants." As the aviation industry matured, a whole battery of instruments was developed as flying aids until we have now reached the point where airline pilots fly on instruments even in crystal clear weather. The analogy for the marketing of packaged merchandise is an apt one and even in "crystal clear marketing weather," it is prudent to be guided by adequate research. This is particularly true in the packaging area where consumer tastes and preferences are most volatile. A body of knowledge is being built in the area of package research (as distinct from research in other phases of marketing) that can be most helpful to the marketer of packaged goods. This is particularly valuable in areas such as instant coffee, cigarettes, beer, etc., where products are substantially alike and where it is the "product image" in the consumer's mind that determines the sale. Depth interviews that help determine the various brand images—the personality profile of the given brand—are most helpful in guiding package planning.

12. "PITFALLS IN PACKAGE RESEARCH"

Probably the major pitfall in package research is basing a decision on incomplete findings. A buy-decision on the part of the consumer is not a simple "I like it" or "I don't like it" kind of determination. Indeed, most consumers, having just made a purchase, cannot really articulate what determined their choice. Apparently, many buy-decisions are motivated from unconscious levels. Adequate package research should consider the following areas:

a. Is the package *noticed* at the point-of-sale (that is, is the package sufficiently powerful to be noticed in a highly competitive market place environment)? If a competitive package is likely to be seen first, your brand is off to a poor start.

b. If noticed, does your package encourage purchase? It would not be difficult to design a package so unusual that it "shouted louder" than all packages around it. However, the results would probably be offensive. The package must not only be seen, it must also motivate the desire to purchase.

c. If purchased, does the package encourage repurchase? (Does the package have the ingredients to build long-term brand loyalty? It must not only be effective in the super market but also in the home. It must be a good working tool of the overall advertising and promotion effort.)

Too often, management will make a decision based on package research that analyzes only a small part of the overall "spectrum" of influence. For example, I have seen decisions based on research as shallow as ratings on legibility and color preferences. Many packages could rate high in these areas and still fail as effective marketing tools.

13. "PACKAGE PLANNING RESPONSIBILITY SHOULD BE HIGH ENOUGH TO ACCOMPLISH THE MISSION*'

More and more companies are realizing that effective package planning requires the full-time responsibility of an experienced executive—usually with a marketing background. This is particularly true in large companies with nationally advertised products with broad product lines. The Director of Package Planning is really a coordinator who guides the development of the package and encourages liaison with product research, packaging suppliers, purchasing, advertising, point-of-sale display and, of course, package design. He is alert to the importance of package innovation, the seeking of new convenience features that can give him a sales advantage. He, of course, is in close touch with the brand manager who must be in rapport with a new package he will be concerned with. It has been our experience that package planning cuts across so many lines of responsibility (i.e., nearly everyone gets in the act) that it requires a highly skilled executive to knit all this activity into an effective result.

14. "DON'T LET YOUR OLD ESTABLISHED BRANDS SLIP"

Many manufacturers are so "new product oriented" that they are not putting the sales effort behind some of their long established older brands—which in terms of dollar volume are still the backbone of the business. When one considers that it costs several million dollars to introduce the average new food product, for instance, and that three out of five of such new products are, by conservative estimates, doomed to failure, it seems poor economics indeed to let a proven money-maker run on bald tires. Especially since it would cost a relatively trifling amount to give the product a new and believable difference from its lower-priced imitators, particularly new packaging which could both stimulate at the point of purchase and provide the basis for exciting new advertising and merchandising.

15. "KEEP YOUR PACKAGING COMMITTEE SMALL"

Many companies have on their packaging committee everyone who might be concerned with some phase of packaging planning. For example, production, purchasing, legal, product research, the brand manager, the advertising agency account executive, etc. A large packaging committee simply can't do the job. The best solution seems to be a small and talented task force headed by the Director of Package Planning who can consult all those interested from time to time and guide the package planning activity to a single packaging recommendation to management. Changes in the market place today are occurring with such rapidity that large, unwieldy committees simply can't do the job.

16. "PACKAGE PLANNING IS A CONTINUOUS ACTIVITY"

There was a time when package changes were so infrequent that when they were accomplished, everyone heaved a sigh of relief and forgot the package until forced to do so again by competition. Package planning is continuous because it involves far more than the graphic aspects or appearance of the package. There is a continual probing for new materials and convenience packaging. There are new products in development that will require a package. Suppliers are coming up with new materials and equipment that require evaluation on the theory that it is better to get there "fustest with the mostest" if you are going to keep and expand your share of the market. It is a good idea to keep probing consumer attitudes and buying habits. What is the brand image of your package in the consumer's mind and how does it rank relative to competition? New packaging ideas should be researched and often sales-tested and this, too, is a continuing activity. One of the great advantages of package planning in continuity is that when the chips are down and you are under urgent stress to produce due to an unforeseen marketing situation, you have the team that can undertake a crash program with the greatest likelihood of success.

17. "DESIGN YOUR PACKAGES AND MERCHANDISERS TOGETHER"

More and more companies are developing special merchandisers in order to display their packages more effectively and to make it easier for the retailer to keep merchandisers full and inventory balanced. It goes without saying that a good merchandiser makes things easier to select and buy on the part of the shopping public. The supermarket abounds with situations where improved merchandisers would help the supermarket operators as well as the public. Baby foods, for example, are particularly hard to stack and are difficult for the housewife to select, carry home and use. It is not easy for the shopper to find the particular electric lamps she wants— size and wattage. On the other hand, the spice manufacturers have done a good job in combining packaging and merchandisers. For some reason, many manufacturers give little thought to the design of merchandisers, relying largely on suppliers to come up with creative solutions. As it becomes increasingly difficult to get to the point-of-sale, more intense effort will be given to designing the package and the merchandiser as a single concept.

18. "BUDGET ENOUGH IN PACKAGE PLANNING TO DO THE JOB"

There was a time when the package planning budget could be zero or very nearly so. Suppliers or the art department of the advertising agency came up with designs for free. Of course, they were not really for free because executive time was spent in evaluating proposed designs and, after all, suppliers and advertising agencies must operate at a profit to stay alive. As the general level of packaging improved and the point-of-sale environment became more competitive, it became apparent that package planning was worthy of a budget commensurate with its contribution to the overall marketing effort. We are now in a period where package planning budgets for nationally advertised brands are substantial and $50,000 to $100,000 for the development of an individual package is no longer considered fabulous or indeed unusual. One thing is for sure—trying to save money in package planning can produce a bigger and more costly backfire than almost any other "economy" you could find. An effective package makes all other marketing efforts that much more effective. There apparently is no ceiling in sight for package planning budgets because each year the research tools become sharper, the materials available for the package become broader and the competitive environment keener. As a result, package planning budgets have only one way to go—and that is up. It is hard to see how one nationally advertised brand can hold its share of the market against another if they are operating under the handicap of a weak package. One of the problems facing management is to determine what size package planning budget makes sense and there are mighty few yardsticks around to help answer this question.

19. "PLAN YOUR LONG-RANGE BRAND EQUITIES"

Most people in today's corporations are concerned with *profits this year.* This is particularly true of brand managers and the advertising agency account executive. After all, if profits slip this year, it might mean their necks. You can hardly blame them for not spending too much time thinking about the brand equity under their responsibility in a long range sense. But long-range planning of a brand equity is important. This is particularly true when it comes to wheeling and dealing. When a brand image is hurt through price cutting or deals or unbelievable advertising claims or a badly designed package, it can very surely hurt long-range profits. A classic example of this was when Packard decided to exploit the favorable brand image associated with the Packard name and bring out a medium priced automobile, seeking a wider market. This decision *did increase* sales and profits the first year or two the new automobiles were introduced, but it undermined the longe-range brand equity until the brand image changed in the consumer's mind from a prestige, high-priced car to just another middle-priced car, and we all know what finally happened to the brand!

20. "IF YOU HAVE A GOOD PACKAGE PLAN-NING CONSULTANT, STICK WITH HIM"

It has been my observation that most manufacturers "hunt and peck" in retaining package designers. They will give one assignment to one designer and, a year later, another assignment to some other designer and then wonder why there is no continuity in their line. By this I do not mean that all packages of a given manufacturer should have a family resemblance. What I do mean is that the package planning effort requires a team working together in continuity and your package consultant is more valuable to you the second year he is with you than the first, and still more valuable five years later. As in any other area in management activity, it takes a time to build an experienced and talented team. There is a better system than "hunt and peck."

William W. Mulvey

W illiam W. Mulvey is Executive Vice President of Cunningham & Walsh. He graduated from Union College, Schenectady, New York, in 1938 and started as a copywriter at Batten, Barton, Durstine & Osborn. He served in creative, account and marketing capacities at Kenyon & Eckhardt and Maxon, Inc., before joining Cunningham & Walsh. At Cunningham & Walsh he is Chairman of the Operations Committee, and member of the Finance Committee, Executive Committee and the Board of Directors.

Some Ideas to Help Young People Succeed

William W. Mulvey

1. Time is precious. To be a successful executive, one must master it. Three hints: (a) before leaving the office at night plan next day's schedule, in detail, by quarter hour, on a sheet of paper large enough to follow easily; (b) when you have a meeting—even a small luncheon meeting—have a *written* agenda, with a copy for each one attending; (c) before you go to see the boss, list the subjects you want to discuss on a slip of paper. Then use it as a guide, thus economizing on his time and yours. Get in and out fast. And edit your words when speaking. When the boss asks you what time it is, don't tell him how to make a watch.

2. An account can't be run successfully without (a) clear understanding and (b) good communications between client and agency. For better understanding, each account should have a Book of Procedures, spelling out client and agency responsibilities. For better communications, each account should operate on a Conference Report

system. This means reporting, in writing, whenever a decision is made in a meeting between client and agency representatives.

3. You have an obligation always to see, or talk to, every media representative who calls. This is an obligation you owe to them, your agency, and yourself.

    And you have a responsibility to see people seeking a job. Just remember—but for the grace of God you would be on the other side of the desk.

    Some friends of mine practically run a one-man employment agency as a hobby. This is a wonderful thing to do. There is simply nothing more rewarding than giving a fellow a lead, or introduction, that results in a job. Particular assistance and encouragement should be given young people who are trying to get their first agency job.

4. Before making your annual presentation—or any major recommendation, for that matter—expose it to all echelons of the client organization. You'll receive helpful suggestions. And— most important—you will have made the executives at operation levels a part of the presentation.

5. From the first day you go to work in an agency, try to give more than is asked of you. If the hours are 9 to 5, work 8:30 to 5:30. If the boss asks for ten headlines, give him fifteen. If you have a point-of-sale piece to devise, go out into the stores on Saturday and see what competition is doing, find out from store managers what is needed. Then create the piece.

    You can't help but make a good impression, *move ahead,* when you give a bit more.

6. This is a high pressure business. You will always be in the position of having to do a number of jobs at the same time. Complete chaos will result unless you learn to organize your mind and time.

   One of the secrets of doing this is to list mentally the jobs in order of importance. Then, to make sure you're not straying from the list, write it out from time-to-time, listing first jobs first.

7. I once gave the same set of sales figures to two different analysts. After studying them a week they each came back with their findings. One chap's findings were ordinary. On the other hand, the other had uncovered many interesting things that helped us quickly to determine marketing strategy.

   The difference was creativity. One had it, the other didn't.

   This is, above all else, a *creative* business. You may start as a writer, as many of us have, and end up an administrator. But always remember—you're a creative man first, no matter what you're doing.

   In running his account, the Account Supervisor is concerned with long-term strategy—this can be, should be, highly creative. The account executive is concerned with day-to-day strategy— this is no less creative.

   Many of the good agency treasurers and comptrollers started as writers. Some of them, such as BBDO's late, great Robley Feland, remained creative. They were creative finance men.

So, stay *creative!*

8. As you develop and succeed in the business, keep in mind one thing above all else: you are only as good as your team.

   The day of the entrepreneur, the one-man-band, is gone. And thank goodness.

   As Captain of the team, your job is to get the others to work together pleasantly, profitably. The more the enthusiasm, the higher the spirit—the better Captain you are.

   Don't lecture; suggest.

   Don't be dogmatic; be open-minded.

   Don't glower; make the job fun.

   Don't be against things; be *for* things—particularly when they're suggestions made by others.

   And when you make a presentation, don't be a prima donna and monopolize it. Make it a complete team operation.

   Clients like to feel they are getting the service of a driving, competent *team,* staffed in depth. And this is as it should be. This is the *modern* way of doing business.

9. The men you work for will mold your future to a great degree. Learn all you can from them. Then put this knowledge to productive use.

   I have been fortunate over the years to have worked for outstanding men. Les Pearl and Charlie Brower at BBDO. Ed Cox at K&E. Mike Mahony at Maxon. Jack Cunningham and Bob Newell at Cunningham & Walsh. Each of them taught me something different. The result was knowledge I would not have acquired without them.

So, study the boss—learn everything you can from him.

10. Learn to make your meetings productive, (a) Open meeting by stating at the very beginning the purpose of the meeting, (b) Encourage others to talk, (c) Set responsibilities, (d) Keep discussion on the track, (e) Keep the meeting short. Most hour meetings can be done in half the time.

11. Spend a certain amount of time each day *thinking.* I use my commuting time for this purpose. This means I have two hours a day, ten hours a week, for thinking, planning, analyzing. And it's been very profitable.

12. To plan is to succeed.

    So, plan. Plan your day. Plan your week. Plan your month. Plan your year. Plan your life.

    This means setting goals for you. It means taking an inventory every so often of assets and liabilities.

    Like all marketing plans, your personal plan should be based on an appraisal of (a) Where you've been, (b) Where you are now, and (c) Where you're going.

    And don't just think it out. *Write* it out.

13. Your mind is working for you all the time, even when you're asleep.

    So, when you're having trouble licking a particularly tough creative problem, forget about it, sleep on it. Then come back to it.

    You'll be surprised how often the answer will appear, seemingly out of the blue. This is known as the power of the subconscious.

14. In making a recommendation, start by spelling out the problem.

    Then list all the possible solutions.

    Next, list the pros and cons of each solution. Then, through the process of elimination, arrive at the solution or plan, recommended.

15. When a fellow is harassed, through overwork, and you have to get a job out, try kidding him into doing the job. This often works more effectively than pleading, cajoling.

    And it *always* works more effectively than trying to argue him into it.

16. There is, unfortunately, a lot of what I call "self-hypnotism" in our business. This is thinking one's own creative idea is better than the other fellow's idea—when it actually isn't.

    Cultivate the ability to analyze the value of ideas. And, by all means, be as critical—be *more* critical—of your own ideas than you are of the ideas of others.

17. I think a lot of so-called "politics" is nothing more than misunderstanding.

    So, when you're in a situation that appears to be political, make an attempt to understand the other fellow and his position. And make sure that he understands your problem. To accomplish this last, there is no better method than the *direct* method. This means going to the chap involved, sitting down with him and talking the misunderstanding out.

18. Agency executives are no longer called on for simply advertising counsel. They must now help in all phases of marketing. Product analysis and planning, sales analysis and planning. Yes, even corporation planning.

So, if you're going to be successful, you must become a well-rounded business man, as well as an advertising man. This means following a consistent reading plan. *Wall Street Journal, Forbes, Fortune, Business Week, U.S. News and World Report.* These are the kinds of publications that can teach you much, when read regularly.

19. Motivation is all important. Some have it, some don't. Those who get to the top have it.

I'm referring to drive. The overwhelming desire to get there, to succeed.

The other day a young account man came to me and asked for a job on an account we haven't even been awarded yet.

About this same time, we asked the members of our young account group to make two or three calls on drug stores on Saturday. This same chap made fourteen calls! Obviously, he has the motivation, the drive, and the desire.

20. Now—you can read and study until doomsday—work twice as hard as anyone else—be three times smarter— and you'll still not make it unless you learn one thing above all else: how to get along with people.

This is the number one rule. If you are one of those people who are psychologically incapable of working pleasantly with people—give up advertising and seek out another profession that is not based so completely on human relations.

John M. Paver

G raduate of Northwestern University with both B.S. and C.E. degrees. After years with Sun Maid Raisin Association, joined Outdoor Advertising Association. Became a "Fellow" of Harvard University's Erskine Bureau of Street Traffic Research. Coauthor of *Trade and Traffic.* Author of *Window Display, Circulation and Market Coverage.* Organizer of Traffic Audit Bureau. Later appointed Managing Director of TAB. Co-inventor of Sills-Paver automatic traffic recorder. Elected President of National Outdoor Advertising Bureau.

A Few Principles
of Human Relations

John M. Power

A few of the principles of Human Relations in Organization which I have learned and used successfully in management over the years:

1. CUSTOMARY PSYCHOLOGICAL REACTIONS OF INDIVIDUALS IN ORGANIZATION.

The energy we put into our jobs is high or low in proportion to our feeling of authorship.

There is positive joy in creative workmanship.

2. RELATIONSHIPS OF SUBORDINATES AND CHIEFS.

Subordinates tend to accept the wishes of their superiors without question.

It is an essential of good management to get out in the ranks and show interest in work and problems. However, this should not interfere with instructions and orders coming through regular managerial channels.

3. ANTICIPATING OR CONTROLLING CONFLICT SITUATIONS.

Autocratic methods at the head of an organization tend to repeat themselves all down the line.

Active participation and personal interest on the part of those who are to carry out a program are essential to its success.

No amount or kind of written material when prepared at higher management levels *can alone* enlist real participation and interest at lower levels.

4. PSYCHOLOGICAL REACTIONS WHEN CHANGES IN ORGANIZATION STRUCTURE ARE BEING CONSIDERED OR ARE BEING INTRODUCED.

In making organization changes it is essential to keep the established group spirit intact and if possible augment it. One's attitude toward a situation has psychic as well as practical (technical-structural) components when making changes.

5. PRINCIPLES FROM THE TRAFFIC AND TRADE RELATIONSHIP.

The increase in mobility of the consumer has given him a freedom and range of market choice that he did not possess before the improvement of transportation facilities—thus making it possible for sellers to draw patronage from far removed buying power—through the use of standardized poster and painted display advertising—"Trades Message to Traffic."

6. The functions of retail trade are closely related to the daily movement of buying power in terms of traffic flow.

7. The space distribution of total traffic forms stable patterns that indicate the daily, habitual movement of population or the total daily buying power-mobility of any market.

8. The time distribution of various classes of traffic creates characteristic and normal patterns resulting from fundamental and stable community habits.

9. There is a close relationship between the quality and quantity of traffic flow and sales of various retail commodities.

General

10. Say it with as few words as is possible.

11. In selling and advertising it is essential to be *so specific, so objective, so positive* that the *obvious* is presented and all questions answered in advance.

12. Never stop moving toward an objective goal or target if it is proven to be a right and proper one.

13. Don't use 24-sheet posters or painted displays unless the proper effort is put into the creation of an idea or image which will present the message to the walking or riding audience in such a manner that it will gather its own audience of the most eyes per dollar of expenditure.

Principles of Window Display Evaluation

14. Window display circulation depends on the movement of near-side pedestrians.

15. Pedestrian movement has relatively stable characteristics and its patterns form the limits of the retail structure of a market.

16. The number of window displays needed for a particular intensity of distribution and a particular intensity of circulation at a given cost per 1000 in any market may be easily determined at an advertiser s desk.

Under General

17. Highly competitive organizations can band together and through cooperation perform (non-competitive) functions in a better fashion, broader in scope, with more efficiency and at less cost than they can perform them separately.

You cannot measure mechanically or technically those actions or functions that deal with variable quantities of the mind or are psychological.

18. Don't be afraid to ask questions.

19. Always live within your income (even though our government doesn't).

20. People are seldom swayed into action on the basis of logic but usually through emotion—that is why in selling and advertising the obvious must be spelled out.

The foregoing are a few of the principles which were derived from examination and discussion of many organization problems brought before Organization Research, Inc., a group of which the writer was a member for over twenty years, where through weekly conferences these various problems of many individuals were solved. The writer has successfully applied these principles (we called them "Nuggets") in the every-day management of the Traffic & Trade Researches, the Army Air Corps, the Traffic Audit Bureau and now in NOAB.

Willard A. Pleuthner

B.S. Degree at Union College in 1924, Honorary LL.D. in 1959. Now Vice-President in New York office of "Management and Marketing Audits Institute." Formerly Vice President in charge of Communications Division, Marketing Department at BBDO. Taught creative advertising courses at University of Buffalo, Columbia and CCNY. Guest lecturer at Harvard Graduate School of Business Administration, MIT, Yale, Princeton, Marquette, Purdue, Army Command School. Introduced Brainstorming in Europe, South and Central America. Author of *Building Up Your Congregation* and *More Power For Your Church.*

A Score and More of Things I've Learned in a Score of Years

Millard a Pleuthner

1. When presenting a new idea to your boss or to your client, remember this proven guide to a more favorable reception: *leave as little as possible up to the imagination of the other person.* Illustrate everything that can be visualized. Spell out everything that can be described. Dramatize anything which will give a dramatic lift to the idea.

    Have prepared answers to all possible questions and objections. Bring along all available marketing facts. Where possible, have estimated costs of testing, and/or the national use of the idea.

    Too often we rush into the boss with a "hot idea." We are hot, he is cold. The result is a lukewarm presentation. The time taken to carry out the above preparations is an essential investment in presenting and selling the idea.

2. It is helpful to practice the technique of proper timing. Learn when your boss has the most receptive mental

climate for new ideas. Maybe this takes place after lunch. Possibly it's after Friday's lunch. Surely it's not when he is head over heels in an involved problem. Maybe this climate prevails just after your boss has closed a big deal or sold a new campaign. Then his mind is more expansive and more open to new ideas. After you learn the "best time" to present new ideas and plan, always make your presentations at that time.

3. Treat your secretary as a partner, not a female unit of automation. Tell her what you are trying to accomplish in serving your boss or client. Describe the personalities to whom you and she are writing. Make them human beings instead of just names.

   Explain the trade terms you use in your dictation.

   Give your secretary presents on her birthday and the anniversary of the date she joined the company. And when you bring your wife a present from a long trip, bring your "office-wife" one too.

   Compliment her for a well-typed plan. And be easy on her Mondays. Almost everyone finds it difficult to adjust to the Monday realities of work after a relaxing, fun weekend.

4. Keep your wife informed on the current history of handling your accounts, Then when you want her opinion on a situation, she has an accumulated background of information on which to give you the best possible advice. Remember that with her intuition, a wife is often in a better position to advise you on some problems . . . even better sometimes than just another man.

5. In direct mail pieces or letters don't forget the stopping power and word-of-mouth value of foreign money. A foreign coin or bill can secure enough extra reading

to justify its low cost. Certain foreign currencies have names which fit in with the appeal of a direct mail piece. For example, you can say:

> Do you have a *yen* to   (and attach a real yen note)
>
> We are *franc* to say   (attach a franc coin)
>
> Do you want to make your *mark* (attach a mark)

Now there are several sources of foreign currency companies which will supply you with these attention-getting devices. One is the Perara Co., of New York. Another is the Royal Coin Co., of New York.

6. The average executive receives his biggest pile of mail on Monday mornings. So when possible, avoid sending your letters, memos, and plans so they are received on the first busy day of the week. On other days your mail has a better opportunity of being given more thorough consideration. It has less competition for attention.

7. There is no substitute for "shopping" retail outlets at regular intervals. Seeing how a client's product is stocked and merchandised (at first-hand) in typical retail outlets, is far better than reading salesmen's reports on the same situation.

    Getting out into stores you can see for yourself: 1) what deals are getting the best display, 2) how many facings your client gets compared to competition, 3) what premiums are being pushed, 4) whose point-of-purchase material is used most widely, 5) new trends in packaging, 6) new items being introduced. So plan to "shop" typical retail outlets at least every other week.

    A personally taken Polaroid picture of what you saw in the store makes your report more complete and more interesting.

8. When designing a point-of-purchase piece, remember to put sales training information on the back side, facing the clerks. This makes them more intelligent sales representatives of your products, at the time when their sales support is needed the most. There is no harm if customers see your sales-training instructions to clerks. They will read it like reading "other people's mail," and be impressed. This use of the back of P.O.P. pieces is worth far more than its low cost.

9. When you're asked a question and don't know the answer, or aren't sure of the answer, say so. Remember that really big men never hesitate to say: "I don't know now—but I'll try to get you the answer." And that's one reason why they are big men.

10. Always have your wife and family try new products as soon as possible. Their first-hand observations will be a help in your thinking on the introductory campaign. It is just as helpful to have your family compare (through use) your products vs. competition.

11. If your company or your client has a stockholder list in the thousands, you have an unusual and extra opportunity to build sales. These people have an additional reason for wanting your products to sell well.

    Properly cultivated, shareholders will do a good job in influencing their friends, neighbors, relatives and favorite retailers.

    Here are just a few of the ways you can build this enthusiastic support.

    a. Have the president write a "welcome letter" to new stock holders.

    b. Use dividend enclosures on new and established products.

    c. Mail sample of new product after trade distribution has been secured.

    d. Send a Christmas box of products.

    e. Enclose with a dividend check a coupon that is good for a discount on a combination of the company's products.

    f. Let the stockholders test potential new products and give you their opinion.

    g. Hold an informal "open house" for stockholders at your regional manufacturing plants.

12. Don't be over-impressed or carried away by the merchandising support of an advertising medium, and let this support be a major   factor in giving it a contract. Support of a medium, in merchandising a   campaign to the trade, is most helpful. But more important are such factors as a) type of audience reached, b) influence of the audience, c) buying power of audience, d) length of time audience is exposed to advertising messages, e) number of times audience is exposed to advertisement, f) editorial climate of publication in relation to products advertised.

13. Always have on your current reading list one book on your business and one self-improvement book. If you only get one usable idea from each, the time-investment is worthwhile. Usually you find several ideas you can use or adapt from each tome.

14. Use your time on commuting trains to catch up on your trade and office reading, or to outline plans. Time on planes is ideal for jotting down notes or next year's plans, projects, etc.

15. In thinking of a new publication campaign, give serious consideration to the use of unusually shaped

ads or unusual space units. Discuss possibilities and availabilities with the space representatives of the media you are considering. Records show that unusually shaped ads can secure above-the-average readership.

For example, a full-page unit of newspaper space used as two lower half pages makes a dominating spread. The regular newspaper editorial materials in the upper half of each page lengthen the exposure of your horizontal spread to the readers.

16. In looking for new ideas, be sure to read stimulating new idea material like *Popular Mechanics,* the "What's New" columns in magazines, and the "New Patents" report in the Saturday issue of the *New York Times.* In reading about these new products, try to think how these new ideas can be adapted to your problems, or can provide new opportunities for your company or your client.

17. When you haven't the time to read the important trade journals, as promptly as you should, ask your secretary to go through them and mark those items of interest to you and your clients.

18. When you are out of town on a long trip, plan ahead to phone your secretary at 10 A.M., after she has opened the mail. Have her read you any mail that needs an immediate answer or action. Then you can tell her what to do over the phone. This prevents wasted time. It makes your "first day back" easier. This telephone check-up can prevent little troubles from becoming big troubles, due to a delay of action.

19. In setting up a "company Communications program," a chart should be made showing each audience ... its size . . . and the general type of material to be sent or offered. In dealing with "Communications" to the brass, much of the material should be *offered,* through a coupon at the

bottom of the description. This prevents your material from cluttering up an executive's mail.

In work on "Company Communications" remember that each major audience should be addressed in its own familiar language, and should only include subjects of interest to that particular audience.

20. Once a year send a check-up questionnaire to all your audiences. Ask them what material they like best and want more of. Ask them what material or subjects not now covered they would like to see included in the "Communications" program.

21. When you are having a conference with your boss or a client, always take along pencil and paper . . . and use them! Write down the other person's suggestions . . . ideas . . . and requests. Don't trust these things to memory, even if you have a good memory . . . and can remember them. Writing down the notes at the meeting impresses the other person that you will take the desired action. This action carries out the promise in that Hammermill Paper Co. slogan . . . "People forget, but paper remembers."

22. Read the trade papers in another field than the one in which you are operating. Every so often, you'll run across an idea on plans in one field which can be adopted or adapted to your industry. For example, you are working on a food account, so you read a good trade paper in the drug field, and you'll run across drug ideas which can also be used in the food field.

23. Always carry paper and pencil with you . . . even in church, for you can never tell when an idea will occur to you, which, if not written down, is apt to be forgotten. That's why people call a pad and pencil an "Idea-Trap." The more you write down ideas, suddenly fed to you "out of the blue," by your subconscious, the more your

subconscious will work for you in problem-solving or idea-developing.

24. Also maintain an "Idea-Bank." In this file folder, you may put clippings of ideas you may want to adopt and use some time in the future.

25. Instead of always writing an executive on his promotion or new job...write his wife instead. Tell her that: "back of every successful executive is a successful wife and mother, and she does such a good job in the home, that her husband has more time to do a better job in his business activities."

26. Always spend time with the second string men in your client's organization. You can never tell when the subordinate will be promoted to be the boss. When you're nice to people on their way up, they'll be nice to you when you're on your way down or just in a status quo situation.

27. In using a coupon or a closing paragraph of suggested action, refer the reader to a specific executive, using his name and title. Many potential respondents like to address their inquiries to an individual, rather than to an impersonal company address, or to a "Department 30-A." The Koppers Co., in Pittsburgh, carries this personalization to the ultimate. They have coupons in their corporate magazine advertisement addressed to "Mr. F. C. Foy, President."

28. When your agency secures a new account (and you're on it), remember one of the greatest sources of information and help in learning this new business are the Media Representatives, who have been calling on the advertiser. They can save you time and trouble in supplying valuable data. This was one of the secrets of the success of Ben Duffy, former President of BBDO.

29. And last, but not least, remember to thank people *in writing* for the helpful things they have done for you ... for the client. . . and for the agency. This little act of appreciation will make you a marked man . . . marked in a way which will assure you more cooperation . . . and more loyalty.

An unusual way to thank people is to use the "Thank-U-Gram" forms which you can get free from the Kimball Foundation, 24 Northcote Drive, St. Louis 17, Missouri.

C. James Proud

Graduated from Medill School of Journalism and Northwestern University in 1928. Spent 12 years as reporter, sports editor, telegraph and city editor of newspapers in Michigan, New York, Pennsylvania and Ohio. Advertising and Public Relations Director of Aeroproducts Division of General Motors, 1940-1945. Joined Advertising Federation of America 1947, became President and General Manager 1957. Director of Advertising Council and member of Advertising Committee of International Chamber of Commerce.

A Hoosier Philosophy

Jim Proud

Psychologists say we are the sum total of all the things we have experienced, and of all the people we have met. If this generalization is even partially true, I must confess to a strong strain of Indiana farm boy philosophy, coupled with an unquenchable faith in the eventual success of organized people, if their cause be just.

Enjoying boyhood on a Northern Indiana farm—before the era of modern conveniences—was one of the nicest things that ever happened to me. Winters were snowbound for weeks on end on that prairie farm, and my brothers and sisters and friends plowed footpaths through the snow banks to the one room schoolhouse where one teacher—usually a relative—reigned with a firm hand and a sharp-edged ruler.

1. All eight grades were taught, quizzed and did their studying in that one room at the behest of the busy teacher, and woe betide the pupil who decided to test the authority of the school mar'm! The era of soft-hearted

teachers and soft-hearted psychologists was yet unheard of, and it was an experience long to be remembered when the no-pound school mistress took 130-pound Johnny by the ear and gave him the caning which he richly deserved. And if Johnny complained at home, his father usually backed up the school mar'm with his leather belt.

2. As I say, we learned to respect authority on those tough rigorous Indiana prairies. And, naturally, the two in our home who had the highest badge of respect and authority were our parents. Never by the greatest stretch of imagination could you have called either of them harsh, but neither were they soft-minded. We learned discipline at age one, accomplished by love and understanding.

   As in every other farm home in those days, each of us had chores to do—wood to cut, to pile behind the old stove, water to pump and reservoir to fill, stables to clean and cows to milk. It was a busy and happy place, winter and summer, fall and spring.

3. I remember one of my mother s favorite sayings, while we were young. "You can't draw water out of an empty well," she would say, and then she'd insist on at least an hour of book-study for each youngster every night. This was her subtle way of encouraging us to fill our mental wells with knowledge for the life ahead. I've always been grateful, for it opened my eyes to the rewards of literature, leading to my career in the newspaper world, to advertising, and finally to the work of a trade association executive.

4. Perhaps the greatest influence on my life came from the great Hoosier authors who have left such a heritage of rich literary effort on the strand of time—Booth Tarkington, Gene Stratton-Porter, James Whitcomb Riley, etc. I can remember leaning up against the old horse barn on the farm and crying as if I had lost my

best friend when news of Riley's death came to our farm. I also remember another great Hoosier favorite—Kin Hubbard, the humorist who wrote *Abe Martin Sez,* which was the forerunner of Will Rogers' beloved witticisms. No one who had the privilege of reading Abe Martin's homely philosophies could ever lack for a sense of humor. The Hoosier "foolosopher" could no more abide stuffed-shirts than could his successor, Will Rogers. It has always seemed a pity to me that no homespun author has arisen to succeed Rogers.

5. I think my father's courage and versatility had much to do with my decision to be a writer. Dad had an indomitable faith in himself and the great Free Enterprise system. Starting from scratch, he and Mother had put together a large acreage of wonderfully fertile Indiana bottom-lands and then he had proceeded to try his hand at various and sundry other businesses-banking, Florida real estate, insurance, gravel digging and even politics.

   Of course, he was not successful in all of these enterprises, but never did he let that dampen his courage or enthusiasm. That is the thing I admired most about him, I suppose. That and his continued faith in the Free Enterprise system.

6. He believed in change and challenge, which is good for all of us, I think. He was always looking for new fields to conquer and new challenges to his interests and ambition. There was never a dull moment in "Life with Father."

   I was interested in reading a feature the other day about Dore Senary, the great Hollywood playwright and director, who suddenly uprooted himself, said "goodbye" to the cinema capital, and is launching a new career on Broadway in mid-life.

Senary, who finds the stage "more fun, more stimulating" than Hollywood, believes "you should shake up your life and change your pattern. It gives you a sense of adventure and renews your drives. And you mustn't wait too long before you do it because caution, timidity and fear will make it impossible for you to ever break away."

I agree with that philosophy as a means of getting the greatest challenge and fun out of life. My father showed me the way by example and I've had fun following a fluid, flexible pattern in my own career. Of course, it is tough on my poor wife and family sometimes, but the challenge and stimulation far outweigh the disadvantages, in my opinion.

7. My four years in Medill School of Journalism at Northwestern University were an exciting and stimulating overture to the main act. Walter Dill Scott was then President of Northwestern and he had contributed as much to the psychology of advertising techniques as probably any one leader. He was a great university president, too, for he not only made students love him, but he had a talent for making rich widows and business tycoons happy to endow our university with their worldly gifts. And that wasn't easy in those depression years.

   Dr. Scott and Northwestern were very kind to me. I learned to write acceptably there, I discovered the fellowship of a fraternity and the advantages of coeducational co-existence. I also learned the disadvantages of stealing red lanterns from street barricades, and have the memory of one night in the Evanston hoosegow to prove all of them.

8. But the greatest lesson I learned at Northwestern was the power of friendship and understanding to overcome obstacles of age and cultural differences. This is a compelling reason for me to exercise the utmost

compassion and understanding for the kittenish pranks of the younger generation today.

Violence and cruelty I cannot understand or condone, however. This is a product of war psychology and mob rule. It is a sickness and should be treated as such.

Despite my fun, I worked hard in the Medill School of Journalism as a reporter for *The Daily Northwestern* and later as an editor. It whetted my enthusiasm so much that I was eager to launch my newspaper career under the direction of Mark P. Haines, publisher of the *Sturgis* (Mich.) *Journal* and a charter member of Sigma Delta Chi, the journalism fraternity, when that organization was founded at De Pauw University.

In Sturgis I met and married my charming wife, who had been a classmate in our big graduating class at Northwestern and whom I had never met until we were thrown together by our first jobs.

But the ephemeral dream of owning your own newspaper some day eventually palls on even the most ambitious newspaperman. That is, unless you happen to be the son of a Medill or a Patterson, obviously qualifying you for "reporter-most-apt-to-succeed" honors.

This is where the need for open-mindedness about a career is most important. After twelve years as a sports editor, telegraph editor and then city editor on dailies from Michigan to New York to Pennsylvania and then to Ohio, I decided that perhaps the newspaper business had not quite been the Mecca I had expected it to be. Besides, I had a wife and son to support, and the advertising business seemed far more lucrative.

9. Again it takes self-confidence and luck to make a leap from one business to another, in spite of the allied nature

of news paper work and advertising. I have always been happy over the broad background of experiences which have come my way, on the farm, as a journalism student and college editor and as a newspaperman and public relations man.

10. Maybe part of my experiences came because I was an introvert converted into an extrovert. By the time I arrived in South Bend High School (Notre Dame's home town had only one high school then) I was a real bookworm. But I saw I had to mix and be a part of the world, if I expected to understand it and have a part in its leadership. Like my Dad, I took a couple of political beatings during my school and college career, but they taught me another lesson—never to be discouraged by setbacks. All this was part of my public relations training.

As a matter of fact, by the time I was made City Editor of the *Dayton Herald,* I was so imbued with public relations that I offered to serve as *The Herald's* newscaster five times weekly on what is now Station WING.

It was fascinating work for a "converted introvert," and I liked to hear old ladies tell me how much they enjoyed my broadcasts.

However, I never have quite forgotten the horror of the night the light bulb burned out in my burlap-lined studio in the Herald building, and I was forced to reconstruct the news of the day by means of a feeble ray of light through the one-inch break in the burlap. I think the *Herald* terminated the remote pick-up experiment a short time after that.

With this strong interest in public relations and advertising, it seemed natural to accept the job of Advertising and Public Relations Director for a General Motors Division headed by an old friend of mine, W. J. "Pete" Blanchard. There followed six busy and hectic war years with this gifted and gracious engineer-inventor. Tragically, he died in an air crash a few years ago.

11. Some of the most important lessons of my life were learned with "Pete" as my tutor. He gave me my greatest lesson in the value of organized effort. World War II was just starting and we had a product which was vital to the war effort. Our greatest problem was that, like Henry Ford's first product, it had never been mass-produced before.

"Pete" Blanchard taught all of us a lesson in loyalty to a cause —and to an individual, himself. Through the sheer dynamics of his own personality, and with the aid of a fine team of technical experts around him, "Pete" took a group of 4,000 strangers and turned them into a highly skilled and single-minded group of loyal friends and war-workers in an amazingly short period of time. We met our schedules and contributed our share to the war effort, with honors.

12. At the end of the war, I decided I was ready for new fields of exploration, like my father before me. And, with "Pete's" blessing, I joined a new company—with much promise. There with I received another lesson—you can't "bank" promises.

13. The old story of good fortune—being at the right place at the right time—proved true again in my own experience, however.

I had been elected president of the Dayton Advertising Club in June of 1946. Elon Borton, new president of the Advertising Federation of America, had made a trip to Dayton to charter the club as a member of AFA. As president of the club, I spent the day with him and he confided that he was looking for an assistant. Early in 1947 I joined the Federation as its first field executive, visiting Advertising Clubs and organizing new ones all over the country.

When I went with AFA in 1947, we had 59 clubs. In 1959, we have 136 Advertising Clubs, 18 national vertical organizations and nearly 1,000 Company Members affiliated with us. We think Fairfax Cone was essentially correct when he said: "AFA Clubs, representing the grass roots of advertising, are potentially the most powerful influence for the good of our industry in Washington, or anywhere else for that matter."

I am convinced that the broad membership of AFA— representing somewhere between 50,000 and 75,000 members—is an unbelievably versatile group of public relations "musicians," if you will, who can do more to raise the standards of advertising and the acceptance of our profession by law-makers and consumers than any other one group.

14. Which leads me to another belief. Advertising is a new profession, in my opinion, because it represents a new way of life—the gearing of our production machinery with our distribution system. While we have not yet been able to decide whether it is an art or a science, there can be no question as to its vital role in sharing America's wealth and production know-how with all the rest of the world.

15. I have come to believe through the years that organizational teamwork is like a great orchestra. Only through a complete and perfect wedding of their combined efforts can the orchestra and its leader rise to the heights of artistic perfection.

Like great musicians, organizational workers are not made overnight. It takes years of learning and familiarity with your profession to cause you to want to give without stint to the upgrading of that calling.

I hope it will come to many of you earlier than it did to me. Life today calls for the most complex orchestration of all human endeavors.

16. Whether America succeeds or fails in the next ten years in "selling" the Free Enterprise system will depend largely on how effectively our leadership—yours and mine—communicates its goals to our nation and to the rest of the world.

As an ex-Indiana farm-boy who believes, I'm betting on your America and mine!

Claude Robinson

A.B., University of Oregon, 1924; M.A. and Ph.D., Columbia University, 1925 and 1932. Financial statistician, 1933-36. Chairman of the Board, Opinion Research Corporation. Co-founder of Gallup & Robinson, Inc. Author of *Straw Votes*.

Keys to
Successful Selling

Claude Robinson

When young people talk about careers, it is easy for them to say they want to be a doctor or a lawyer or a musician, but it is not too socially acceptable to say they aspire to be a salesman. Salesmen, to be sure, are among the best paid professional men, which means that they possess talents that are limited in supply, but the image of the salesman in today's society is not a very flattering one. A salesman is thought to be a good Joe—personality boy, an extrovert who doesn't think too deeply on any subject, a hard drinker and a devotee of "whoopee."

A salesman's job is to deal with people; so, quite obviously, he must have a liking for people and an ability to understand them. But there is nothing superficial about this kind of assignment. On the contrary, salesmanship represents one of the greatest professional challenges in our society today, calling on personal talents of high order—clear-thinking, industry, conviction and character.

1. Correctly defined, a salesman is a problem solver. It is the salesman's business to study other people's problems and furnish answers for them, or show people how they

can satisfy needs, desires, aspirations or ambitions. A good salesman works for his clients, takes care of them, sees to it that they have the best-in short, helps them solve problems. Harry Bullis of General Mills put salesmanship on the proper moral plane when he told a convention of Northwestern Life Insurance representatives:

"When I go out in the morning, I don't ask: 'How many sales will I make today?' I ask, 'How many people can I help today?'"

When a salesman believes in his heart that he has ways to help people, he can take the brush-off and the turn-down that are a part of salesmanship without deflation of his ego. A good salesman, convinced of the Tightness of his cause, sees a turn-down not as a defeat, but as a challenge.

Many people think there is a mystique of salesmanship that is inexplainable. No one, of course, will ever be able completely to fathom the human personality and account for all of its vagaries, but, actually, there is nothing very mysterious about the art of selling.

2. To begin with, it is always desirable to have a good product that meets the needs of the prospects and that has competitive advantages. Good salesmanship depends heavily on repeat business. If the prospect is sold once, but doesn't like the product and refuses to buy again, it will prove to be costly selling. The only way a successful company like Procter and Gamble can afford its lavish expenditures on advertising is that for most new sales it gets one or more repeat purchases.

3. The second necessity in selling is to have keen insight into the prospect's problems, needs or desires. This is not easy to come by. It takes hard, concentrated study and lots of imagination to project oneself into the other man's world and view things as he sees them, feel his

concerns, understand his prejudices, and know his goals. But there can be no compromise on this point. Either the salesman knows his prospect and his prospect's business or he cannot expect to sell.

3. The third requirement in successful selling is activity. If one has a good product that will help people, it is necessary to let them know about it. The more people who hear the good news, the greater the number of sales. In mail-order selling, sales from activity can be predicted with astonishing accuracy. In selling through mass media, the movement of merchandise is ordinarily limited to the tonnage or dollars spent. Likewise, in personal selling, the greater the number of calls, the more sales will be made. Activity varies in effectiveness, depending on the quality of sales presentation, but at any given level of presentation, sales will closely correlate with activity.

4. The fourth requirement in successful selling is demonstration. It is not only necessary to tell a prospect that your product is good, but show him how it works, how it has worked for others, how it can work for him, and why it works that way. Simple assertion about a product is weak sell; assertion together with demonstration is hard sell.

5. The fifth key to successful selling, of course, is repetition. People do not necessarily get the salesman's message in one statement or in one exposure. Hence the good salesman repeats his main points several times in one presentation, and makes as many presentations as necessary to effect a sale. In mass selling through space advertising, the principle of repetition is observed by repeating the message in the headline, the illustration and the copy. In all media, repetition is achieved by presenting the same sales arguments with variation in different ads or commercials.

6. The sixth key in selling is what I call "mental work." People are busy and there is much competition for everyone's time. It is necessary to conserve energy; hence most folks will not labor to get a sales message. The work must be done by the presenter. The rule of mental work is: "The more work required of the respondent, the less he will register on your message. The less work required of the respondent, the more he will register on your message."

7. All of us are familiar with the problem of mental work. We like to have ideas presented to us simply, colorfully, clearly, de-monstrably, so that we can get the point without having to accelerate our nerve impulses. The salesman or communicator must have considerable understanding of this roadblock in communication if he is to eliminate it from his presentations. High symbolism, coined words, disorderly layout and lack of thesis are some examples of communication involving mental work.

8. In personal selling, the presenter usually knows when his prospect is overcome by mental work and fails to get the point. In mass selling through ads and commercials mental work must be avoided in the copy and illustration or in what is said and shown, for messages that are not crystal clear score very low in communications and sales efficiency.

    So here are six keys to success in practical selling— good product, consumer benefit, activity, demonstration, repetition and the avoidance of mental work. These six keys, interestingly enough, are widely applicable not only to the selling of a product but also to communications generally and to leadership.

    If you wish to communicate successfully to a mass audience, then it is necessary to have something to say (i.e., a good product), talk to the other fellow's interest, demonstrate your points, repeat them, make your thesis clear, and talk to as many people as need be.

If you are a community or political leader, you are, in fact, offering a leadership program or a set of ideas "for sale." Your success or failure depends on what people, and how many, "buy" your program or your philosophy. So, once again, the six keys come into play: good program or worthy ideas, interpreted in terms of the other fellow's interest, demonstrated or proved, repeated, clearly stated and communicated to as many people as is necessary for your purpose.

Much time, energy and money is wasted in selling. In our research we constantly see two television commercials where one sells three times as effectively as the other; or two ads where one will have an audience ten times as big as the other. In personal salesmanship, too, we see one man knocking on doors, getting orders, and the other knocking on doors or visiting offices and coming home empty-handed. What accounts for the difference? We will never know the complete answer because human nature is infinitely complex, but try the six keys described above. You will be gratified by the results.

Hal Stebbins

❝Mr. Advertising Man of the West." Competent judges consider him one of America's top-tier creative men. *Printers' Ink* calls him "One of the most brilliant thinkers in advertising—and one of the most articulate." Co-founder of Honig-Cooper, San Francisco. Later president, Erwin, Wasey and Company of the Pacific Coast. Since 1950 head of his own national agency in Los Angeles. He has personally written more than a hundred million dollars' worth of advertising. Prolific writer. Dynamic speaker. University lecturer. Author of a half-dozen books. His *Copy Capsules* (McGraw-Hill) voted "one of 50 best business books of the year.

No Substitute for "Imagineering"

1. In writing, the way to add is to subtract. The man who can say things without saying them is a great copy writer.

2. Don't try to write—just try to say something. And say it with passionate conviction. If you don't believe it, don't say it. The man who writes tongue-in-cheek forgets that the reader feels it—instantly and instinctively. For, if every man paints his own portrait, every copy man writes his own biography when he writes the biography of a product or service.

3. What can you do with a story you think dishwater-dull? You an dig deep for the drama that's in the product. It's there—if he product is there. You remember that the surface of society, like that of the sea, is in perpetual motion. The world changes— constantly. So you change. You use *perpetual emotion.* You use cross-pollination. You adopt or adapt. You lengthen or lessen. You put the common in uncommon environment. If nothing else, you

throw new light on an old scene—and thus give it new life, new interest, new color, new imagery.

4. Always sit on this three-legged stool: *First—facts!* You have to know before you go. *Second—emotion!* To move products you must move people. *Third—technique!* Never let the manner detract from the matter.

5. Don't hesitate to animate inanimate things. We talk about the *ears* of a cup; the *teeth* of a saw; the *legs* of a table; the *elbow* of a pipe; the *head* of a hammer; the *soft shoulders* of a road; the brow of a hill; the week of the woods.

   Chesterton tells us of a farm girl who, at first sight of the sea, was asked to describe it. She said it made her think of "a giant cauliflower." Whether you like cauliflower or not, you have to agree it is an apt analogy—phrased in language native to her.

   Thus, when you call a floor "tired" you've made a dead thing live. Robert Louis Stevenson was a master at this. He talked about "the desert's hot and dusty face." He wrote: "The mountain rose before us" . . . "the leaves danced in the wind." So keep your copy *on the move*—by using words that live and breathe. Woo verbs. Jilt adjectives. For adjectives are "fillers"— not "feelers."

6. Don't confuse a short sentence with a choppy one. It takes real surgery to shorten a ligament; not mere snipping. Don't say, "One of the world's greatest hotels." Say, "One of the world's great hotels." Less sugar on the superlative makes it sweeter.

7. It is very easy to produce advertising that is safe. It is not so easy to produce advertising that is not only safe but seductive. You don't do it with dots and dashes, with popeye exclamation points. You do it by putting quiet

thunder into what you say. You do it with lightning-rod ideas that hit people where they live—in their emotional centers. And you always remember that people don't think with their "thinkers" but with their "feelers"—their emotions.

8. Advertising is the art of communication. But before you can *communicate* you must *commune*—with people, with Nature, with the world around you, with yourself. The truly creative mind is interested in anything and everything. The more catholic your interests, the richer your mental granary—the greater inner sources you can tap. Perennial hunger is the key to a full mind. Your stomach can get full, your mind never.

9. If I have a "B-Complex" for Copy Writers it is this: Be human. Be simple. Be sincere. Be specific. Be informative. Be authoritative. Be enthusiastic. Be sure you're understood. And, above all, be believable.

10. Boiled down to its bones, the Art of Selling is the Art of Plain Talk. There are those who decry this emphasis on simple language; who contend that, as a nation, we are becoming more literate—hence more intelligent; and that to fill our advertising with one- and two-syllable words is stupid and archaic. Then we have our ultra-moderns, the rash rebels who join The Cult of Unintelligibility. These nose-tilted lads have my blessing—and my pity. They will find that Great Men often are misunderstood but not Great Copy Writers. It is Cervantes, I believe, who tells us, "The pen is the tongue of the mind." Perhaps this explains why so many pen-pushers go in for tongue-twisters. It is easier to talk than to talk sense; and sometimes easier to be confusing than to be clear.

11. Copy isn't words. And it isn't pictures. Copy is what you *do* with what you *have*. Copy is what you use to make people be have—the way you want them to. You can't *change* people; but you can *channel* them—your way. That's why it is more important to cultivate people than to cultivate words. For the answer to the question: "What makes people *buy?*" is another question: "What makes people *people?*"

12. Copy writers should enjoy the Freedom of the Sees. They should see, feel, taste, touch, the things they write about *before* they write. They should be fugitives from the desk-gang and revel in it. They should get out and get under and see for themselves. They should drink in their impressions *first-hand* instead of getting them from mumbo-jumbo Conference Reports. They are writers, not robots. They should have a nose for news, and they should translate that news into something the reader wants more than the money it costs.

13. A good advertising man must be a romanticist on top and a realist at bottom. He must have a sense of imagery harnessed to a sense of practicality. He must be a good city editor Burbanked with a cash-register complex. He must be a humanist, a realist, a register-ringer— all in one. That may sound like a high-grade hybrid but that's it: a mental merger, a blissful blend, of Star Dust and Pay Dirt.

What's more, a good advertising man must have a chronic, conscious curiosity about *everything*. He is dealing with the stuff of life. Therefore he should go through life with his hand, as well as his head, in the air. He should ask questions constantly. He should probe not only *what* but *why.*

And please remember what I have said to scores of advertising audiences across the nation: Advertising is a *young mind's* business, not a *young man's* business. It isn't how old you are— it's how bold you are! How resourceful and resilient; how courageous and contagious!

14. You hear endless debate on whether advertising is a business or a profession. This has always struck me as silly semantics—as an academic waste of time. Advertising is an ad-mixture of business and profession. It is a burgeoning art that—with widening understanding and application—will some day achieve the status of a science. But the day will never arrive—in spite of all the electronic genius in the world—when IBM lightning-research and robot writers will take over. For the human equation always transcends the mathematical. Advertising deals with the alchemy of the human heart and mind. That's why you can't reduce it to a mathematical formula. You can't measure the human equation with test tubes or tape measures, with millines or micrometers. The chemistry of *life* has everything to do with the chemistry of *sales.*

15. No business or profession in the world enables a man to use his eyes, his ears, his God-given brain and his extra-sensory perception, to the same degree and extent as advertising. Nor do I know any business or profession that offers such genuine challenge—such play for creative imagination—such opportunity to influence human behavior through the dissemination of information and ideas.

Everything that happens or doesn't happen—everything you see or hear—everything you read or remember—is grist for the mill of the advertising mind. It's there—up in the air. All you need are the antennae—to capture it and make it yours. It's all a matter of exposure and absorption. It's what *your mind* does with what funnels through your eyes and ears.

Summed up and simmered down, an advertising man is a man who takes *facts* and translates them into *ideas;* translates these ideas into *emotions;* translates these emotions into *people;* translates these people into *sales.*

16. In spite of all the hubbub you hear today, the *raison d'être* of the advertising agency has not basically changed. Many refinements of service have been added. It is no longer a One Horse Shay that begins and ends with copy. It taps many fields, recruits many skills, integrates many functions. But, so long as markets are made up of people—and people are made up of human behavior—the advertising agency will continue to be a *creative mechanism* with copy as its core.

And when I say "copy" I don't mean just words. I mean *everything* that goes into the space or time you buy— including the marketing strategy behind it. The primary function of the advertising agency then, as now, will be *to produce advertising that moves 'products by moving people.*

So let's not be carried away by foolish fads, by tricks and artifice. Let's stick to the truth—*but make that truth exciting.* Let's use research as a guide, not as a god. Let's be on a still hunt for the new and different, the fresh and unorthodox. But, in the process, let's stick to the basics, the fundamentals, the substance and sinew, of advertising.

17. I have never forgotten what Arthur Brisbane told me— many years back—when I asked for editorial support of the Hearst Press on National Prune Week. I showed him the series I had prepared for the California Prune and Apricot Growers—the first national venture of Sunsweet Prunes into newspapers. I explained the Stebbins Calomel-and-Nujol Technique: big ads to dynamite, little ads to lubricate. He took in the whole show in one swift

glance. Then, pointing to the little fellows, he said: "Hal, I don't like those." "What's the matter with them?" I parried. "There's nothing the matter with the copy," he answered. "The ads are just too small. *It's like winking at a girl in the dark—you know you're doing it but she doesn't.*"

18. In advertising, there is no substitute for what has been aptly termed "Imagineering." It means shunning the usual, the commonplace, and the mediocre. It means digging into the subsoil of your mind—and using plenty of cross-pollination. It means fewer Word Factories, more Idea Factories. I know it's not easy. Being human, we spend a lot of time *avoiding* the labor of thought. But it is richly rewarding. And the odd thing about it is this: once you set up this mental mechanism and keep feeding it the anti-sterility Vitamin E called Enthusiasm, you no longer hoard ideas. For, the more you radiate, the more you germinate.

19. The creative process is a dual process. You *build up* by imagination. You *tear down* by analysis. You sift and sort. You select and reject. Then you wait for what Physiologist Gerard calls "the arrival of the fittest."

20. Begin at the end: the way the advertisement will look to the reader, not the writer.

Milton J. Sutter

D irector of Traffic-Production Dept., Cunningham & Walsh, Inc. He has served continuously since 1926 in Agency Production with Cunningham & Walsh and its predecessor, Newell-Emmett Co. Former member and vice chairman of AAAA Standing Mechanical Committee. Chairman of the Mechanical Production Session of the Eastern Annual Conference of AAAA's. Presented Advertising Agency viewpoint at 1957 Convention of American Photoengravers Association. Serving on Customer Relations Committee of the Gravure Technical Association. Member of Advertising Agency Production Club of N.Y. Author of numerous articles on production and traffic.

26 Production Tips

1. Trade up *quality,* trade down inferiority. White space, especially in terms of today's rates, is too costly except for materials of top-grade superiority.

2. Your traffic-production procedure or system may be the best b*ut* it is only as good as the strength of the authority behind it. If anemic, get it beefed up!

3. Suppliers are your operation's backbone. Don't just visit your suppliers—haunt their plants. Investigate, analyze and evaluate each one's manpower, equipment, service, product, progressiveness and ethics. Be selective in your choices, yet use as many sources as you require. This is one way you get the broad picture and cross-check on quality, service and costs you're accountable for.

4. A good production man will be recognized readily by the lack of shine on the seat of his pants. This is indicative of his trek through engraving plant, press rooms, electro

foundries and type shops. It is here he gets the first-hand knowledge, know-how and experience so essential to his job.

4. Try to obtain the basic production training in an agency where you can assimilate all the phases in the operation, where you can handle the ads from engraving, to type specifying and casting, through electrotypes and print detail. You'll make a better *specialist* if you choose, having spent sufficient time and having the proper background to understand and correlate all functions of graphic arts.

5. If you dislike or can't take detail, stay away from production or traffic.

6. Do the right job at the beginning and the end result will be satisfactory. This is one very important reason why mechanical requirements established and enforced by publications to up grade printing quality, should be followed faithfully by all connected with the creation, preparation and production of advertising.

7. Whoever said "Relax, the plates are finished and shipped" could never have been a production man. How well the publications print the ads is the most important and critical period to the P.M. He can afford to relax only after he checks the book and sees the printed facsimile.

8. Don't be a one-man operator. Ask for and use freely the help and skills of your fellow workers on the staff. They'll be more than willing to aid in any dilemma. You, too, will have ample opportunity to reciprocate by sharing your knowledge and resources when the need arises.

9. The graphic arts is a constantly moving business which is progressing at the fastest pace in its history. In order to keep abreast of the developments it is important that all production personnel be constantly alert and aware of these advances.

Attendance at conventions, educational programs and seminars sponsored by the various industries, associations and production clubs is a requisite. Time is the only *'prerequisite*. Most are given free or at nominal cost.

10. When running an advertisement with a very light overall half-tone or tinted background in newspapers it is better to sacrifice position or give an option of days in order to assure and obtain second impression printing. The effect will be a cleaner printed advertisement without the strikethrough which would have been the result on a first impression page. This can be re quested in your order to the paper.

11. Deal directly with the person or persons involved in the job. Insist on getting and giving written instructions. Many important instructions are distorted, garbled or lost by third or fourth party interpretations.

12. Production is a creative function in the agency. The P.M. by his knowledge of availability, adaptability and practicality of various processes and methods is able to help interpret and translate the ideas, artwork and copy of art director, artist and copywriter for use in print media. For instance, the suggestion of the use of a fifth press-cylinder to obtain a special color is a case in point. The analysis of a full-color job to obtain practical, satisfactory print results is another. The P.M. had a very important creative share in the development of Hi-Fi color-gravure printing of inserts for newspapers.

13. There is no better way to improve one's store of knowledge than to take, *regularly,* copies of national magazines and go through them observing, studying and analyzing the components making up the ads. Observe how they were handled. Figure how you would have performed the job to get better results. Recognize the

good and practical characteristics; note the dangers and pitfalls to avoid. Make them case histories by checking your analysis with the agency P.M. who handled the ads.

14. ubscribe to the many excellent trade magazines covering the graphic arts field. Read, study and file for future reference all the brochures and bulletins put out by the American Photo-engravers Association, the International Association of Electrotypers & Stereotypers, the Advertising Typographers Association of America, the Gravure Technical Association, the Lithographers Association, the 4-A's, as well as technical books by well-known experts.

15. Study the requirements and problems from all practical angles before you hand out advice or write the order. Hasty decisions may mean an expensive charge-off. There may be a better, speedier or more economical way.

16. Do you know you can get a degree in advertising production? Five years ago you couldn't. But now courses are available at N.Y.C. Community College of Applied Arts and Sciences in Brooklyn which lead to an A.A.S. in Advertising Production Management. Production men aided and abetted in developing the necessary curricula. Through the Advertising Agency Production Club of N.Y. scholarships and grants-in-aid are being made available to deserving students. This is not a token venture, for the fund has grown to over $2,000 annually through contributions from suppliers and agencies.

17. Always have available the tools of your profession. Dictionary, T-square, triangle, pica rule, magnifying glass, reducing glass and depth gauge. Be sure you know how and when to use them. These items are essential for

checking and squaring layouts and sizes; to cast, specify and proof-read type; to be able to study minutely the dot formations and characteristics, and depth of plates.

18. Don't be over-zealous in using or advocating a new processor method. Make your recommendation *only* after demonstrated, proved results and studied care in investigation. Thus you will avoid anxious, costly and embarrassing errors.

19. Be wary of giving "horseback," "quickie" *guess-ti-mates* from sketchy tissues or verbal job descriptions. They have a way of becoming inadequate estimates to which you may be held. Have a form which itemizes all the particulars needed to furnish the job right down to sales tax and delivery charges. In any event, make sure the estimate is a complete and written one. Often it is wiser to overestimate than to err by underestimating.

20. Copy should be set to be read. Help it do so by adhering to the yardstick and rules of legibility and good taste set up by experienced hands. Type setting only for design won't do the job intended by the author. Combine readability and design in one package. Study the ways contemporaries are doing this and what the past masters of type did. You'll be the gainer. Be especially aware of surprinted and reverse type requirements. Avoid faces with thin connectors and contrasty features; settle on more weighted and uniform type designs.

21. Paper is basic to print media. The better the understanding of this factor, the better and more efficient will be the correlation of paper, ink and print. Acquaint yourself with paper in all its components; its manufacture, finishes, opacity, sizes, limitations, availability and economy. Again turn to the folders, booklets and brochures available from paper makers. Visit paper plants when and whenever opportunity arises.

22. Ask the electrotyper to furnish you with a proof from each of the plates with identification of addressee or of the pattern plates from which mats are being pulled. By checking these proofs you can quickly ascertain where each plate went and what its pre-shipping condition was.

23. Keep your eye on DuPont's Photopolymer engraving system. It is capable of producing engravings from print to finished plate in approximately fifteen minutes' time. Successful, in-plant, field-testing programs have been under way for some time. Combined with the step-and-repeat method of print copying, the future could witness a duplicate plate making miracle.

24. In obtaining approval of artwork for 24-sheet posters before release to the lithographer I have resorted to using a transparency in lieu of the usual hand-painted copying of the design. The transparency is viewed at full 24-sheet size in the lithographer's projection room. Here size, placement and relation of the components with each other can be seen in full scale. Of course, we do not judge color values of the pictorial elements here. After all, it is the lithographer s responsibility to give facsimile repro duction of the art. A transparency saves time since it can be processed in a day or two whereas the hand-painted job may take from one to two weeks. As a result it is more economical, since the cost of the ektachrome is only a fraction of the cost of a paint job.

25. Ask the lithographer to furnish a sheet layout of your poster. This will indicate how he plans to print and cut the sheets that will make up the design. Often alternate ways can be suggested to eliminate cutting through small elements or features, such as through the eye, etc. Horizontal cuts through lettering should be minimized or avoided wherever possible. It may require only a slight vertical shift above or below the cut.

26. Many publications offer a range of standard inks in various shades. Confronted with that elusive match of art, product or package it may be helpful and necessary to depart from the usual colors to obtain the desired result. Check with the publications' ink books; consult with them and your engraver.

It is amazing how readily the rush of a job can be *forgotten* when the bills arrive or the end results are unsatisfactory. Eliminate these irritating factors by pre-planning. Better understanding plus more complete knowledge of each other's problems, requirements and limitations is mandatory. It will result in better, more harmonious relationships.

Accept the challenge of the unusual. You'll discover novel and perhaps untried ways in solving the problem.

William Taubin

B orn in New York. Attended Parsons School of Design in N.Y. Early A.D. experience was with several department stores such as Abraham and Straus and Franklin Simon. A.D. at Douglas D. Simon, Inc., and at present with Doyle, Dane, Bernbach. Has been responsible for several campaigns such as El Al Israel Airlines, Chem-strand Nylon, Buxton, Woman's Day, Levy's, Ancient Age, etc. Holds Art Director Club medals, AIGA awards.

And Finally,
Be Dedicated

William Jauler

The real secret of success is that there is no secret of success. At least, not in the advertising business.

I now have spent about twenty years in the advertising business. Out of the twenty, some have been wonderful years, some have been awfully lean years, some have been frustrating ones. Somehow I have found myself taking "two steps forward, one step back." If I can keep you from taking some of the backward steps, then perhaps this chapter will be worth the time you spend in reading it.

First of all, like many young people starting out, I followed the style of my idol of that period.

1. I've found from experience that to follow someone else's style can lead you completely up a blind alley. These people understand their own style and they know what they're doing. To follow the leads of these people, even though they may be the best in the business, is basically unsound. You may learn the idol's technique so well that when he has dropped that style or technique, you're

stuck with it. To become so enamored of a style—and not the *substance* of it—can prove to be disastrous.

2. By all means, develop a technique of your own, crude or imperfect though it may be. And by all means, don't get "married" to one style. It may become a ball and chain. I've seen this happen to many men in the business: they get a wonderful technique and they become so wedded to it that they can no longer change.

3. Our business is a constantly shifting, constantly changing one. If you want to survive and grow in it, you must be flexible enough to shift all the time. Those who aren't flexible become sterile. Where do your best ideas come from?

4. First, let me tell you where they *don't* come from. The freshest, the most original ideas *don't* come from thumbing through copies of Graphics or Art Director's Annuals.

5. Nor do they come from seminars. Too many young people (sometimes, even seasoned art directors) go to seminars hoping that some famous art director is going to say some precious word that will give them "the answer." He doesn't. He can't. He isn't even trying to. He is only offering his own experiences as another means for exploring. And that's good and worthwhile. But he expects you to do the exploring and finding out for yourself. *In* yourself. Your best ideas will come from life around you. From people's faces in the subway. From the newspapers. From wonderful books you read. From things you observe in the movies and in plays. And the closer to real life the better; the humbler the better.

6. Try to soak up everything you see, everything you hear. Become a sponge of experiences; don't become a sponger.

7. You will find that something which moved you deeply ten or twenty years ago will suddenly pop into your mind to provide the ideal solution to a current problem. It must come from deep inside you; from your own guts. And then the ad will come to life for other people.

8. When you're working in the advertising business, you must try to reach the reader through experiences he recognizes, knows and enjoys. This is the way I work. I try not to be esoteric. The consumer doesn't respond to art that's just talking to itself instead of talking to him. I try to use humor that anyone can understand and enjoy— whether it's a cab driver or a highly sophisticated person.

9. Another don't. Don't get buried in the graveyard of technique, beautiful though it may be. Every day you will be called upon to make decisions between whether an ad is going to work—or just be a decorative piece.

    For instance, take the question of typography and readability. I have seen many ads that were graphically beautiful, but I'll be damned if I could read them. And if type can't be read easily (after all, in an ad that is its primary function), then it shows poor art direction, no matter how beautiful it may look to your fellow practitioners. I try to use this rule of thumb: if I don't find type inviting to read *myself,* then I can't expect a consumer (who certainly isn't standing around waiting for the message) to take the trouble to read it.

10. Advertising is an art, but it isn't an outlet for frustrated painters. It's not art for art's sake. This has taken me many years to lean.

    So examine yourself as an art student very carefully. And don't, for goodness' sake, go into advertising if painting and fine art are really your true loves. Don't let yourself in for years and years of frustration trying to make great paintings out of ads. Because it just won't work.

Unfortunately, there are too many art directors in the business who feel the desire to do a painting to "cleanse their souls" of what they feel is a prostitution of their art.

11. It took me all these years to learn what Bill Bernbach taught me in a few months: the only function of advertising is to sell. And if what we do, as artists, helps to sell the product, then we have done our job. Many successful ads, of course, *are* beautiful. But if it's beautiful and doesn't sell, it's a failure nevertheless. And this, dear reader, took me many, many years of wandering in the advertising business to learn. If you're lucky enough, maybe you'll come across a Bill Bernbach yourself early in your career, and save yourself a lot of anguish.

12. Don't hesitate to break the rules. If everyone heads east, then *you* go west.

    Let me give you an example: the El Al Israel Airlines' sales-winning and prize-winning ad—the one with the headline, "On December 23rd, the Atlantic Ocean will become 20% smaller," that showed a piece being torn off the Atlantic Ocean.

    At that time, people in the field were saying, "Oh, you can't show such ominous-looking ocean. People will be afraid to travel by air. It just isn't done."

    Nevertheless, this turned out to be one of the really great successes in airline advertising history.

13. Many people in our field are so busy thinking what the people won't like, or will be shocked by, that they frequently miss making contact entirely. And the reason is that they've never really been of the people, never really understood them.

14. Now two big *do's*. Try to get in with a good agency. Especially the agency you start with. One or two years at the beginning of your career under the right boss can pay off in many

thousands of dollars of increased earnings later on. If necessary, take a lower position than you might get elsewhere, if it means that you can get in with a good organization. Even work for peanuts. In the long run, you'll be ahead.

15. And finally, be dedicated to your work. I know it may sound corny, but dedication pays off in personal satisfaction as well as in money.

Ivan Veit

Ivan Veit, born May 31, 1908, in New York City, was graduated from Columbia in 1928, and went immediately to work for the New *York Times*. Started as Classified ad-taker, became Promotion Manager in 1932, Assistant Business Manager in charge of Promotion and Circulation in 1957. Married to Sylvia Lippman in 1930, two children.

There's No End to Learning

1. It is hard to think of any absolute rules in advertising—things that must never be done or always done. The advertising man must always remember the diversity of his calling in order to keep himself from fossilizing. Nevertheless, he must proceed from day to day as if certain ultimate rules *do* exist, meaning the things his own taste and judgment tell him are right. Only in this way can his work or the work of others under his supervision have consistency, continuity and integrity. Practice unsupported by theory is an empty thing. It is necessary to be open-minded and flexible, but behind it all must be a hard set of guiding principles. Someone else may do as well or better with different principles, but that is no reason to be unfaithful to your own.

2. The quality of advertising varies inversely with the number of people who must see it and approve it in advance of publication. Multiple editors nibble

away character, style, point of view, from any advertising. The assumption that any vice-president, comptroller or lawyer is also a good advertising man is unfortunately false. For the best advertisements, put a competent man in charge and leave him alone. He may err in individual instances but over a whole campaign or program, he'll come out far ahead of any blue-pencil team.

3. On any list of factors that keep advertisements from turning out as well as they might, high priority would have to be given to the universal tendency to create and produce at the last possible minute before deadline. Sometimes the spur of necessity may stimulate inspiration, but much more often the hasty product is quite undistinguished. Under pressure of time, the just passable gets approval, design and production are subject to short cuts and compromise, merchandising is slighted. Skilled professionals can turn out ads at high speed—but not their best. Is there a good way to avoid this "last-minute" peril? Only one—a complex reversal and overhaul of human nature.

4. The universal tendency is to discontinue and discard advertising themes long before their effectiveness has been exhausted. Having seen copy, layouts, proofs and finishes several times on each ad, the creative man becomes jaded before the public has even become aware of his campaign. In the restless urge for frequent change, we often find ourselves retiring a first-rate idea in its prime, just to titillate the management or the client with ''something different.''

5. "Get rid of detail—delegate everything you can." This is the fashionable philosophy in business today. This worthy objective is fine for chairmen of the board, presidents, executive vice-presidents and other clean-

desk boys. But not for advertising men. A good ad is the result of many details, subtly and carefully blended — the turn of a phrase, a shift in layout, an adjustment of type, a change in color, an intensification of schedule. Divorce yourself from detail and you've lost control of the end product.

6. It's a good thing for every creative man to have at least a small amount of routine work to do—proofs to read, schedules to be checked and the like. Creativity is an intermittent process. No one burns with that hard and gem-like flame straight through from nine to five. A few routine chores are far better than staring .out the window to loosen a man up for the next surge of ideas.

7. Don't overload an advertising program with too many different assignments. There is infinity of things you *could* be doing at any given moment, but only a few can be worthily handled at a time. Try to do everything and you accomplish nothing.

8. No matter how good it is of itself, any mailing piece will get a better reception if it is accompanied by a covering note, memo or brief letter. It gives you a chance to tell the customer quickly what you are up to and to warm up his approach to the mailing piece itself.

9. It takes young men a long time to learn the significance of the fable of the hare and the tortoise. Vigorous and impatient, they like to see innovations installed, reforms adopted and methods revolutionized over night and are aggrieved when their obviously meritorious ideas meet resistance. If they are wise, they soon perceive that "easy does it" is the best technique, gets there fastest in the long run—and with fewer costly mistakes.

10. Most people have a creative potential far above their normal day-to-day level. The problem is to help them tap this natural reservoir. How you do it depends on the man, of course, but one way is to give him a feeling of accomplishment by noting and praising the good things he does. Then set a lofty standard and seek his help in achieving it. You'll find that thus stimulated he'll gladly join you in attempting to scale Mt. Everest when, by himself, he might be discouraged by yonder hill.

11. A lot of time is wasted trying to expand one-shot ideas into full-fledged campaigns. Some really brilliant ideas are good for only one or two ads and then peter out. If you need a 13- or 26-time campaign, the sooner you get out of this kind of dead-end and start afresh, the better.

12. The reader is a lot smarter than most of us think. Somehow he can tell when an ad has honest substance and when it is all tricks and technique. He may *comment* on the cleverness of an ad, but he *responds* to honesty and sincerity. Virtuosity is a great asset for the creative man, but only when it is in harness and under control. By itself, it has little value.

13. This is the heyday of the group, the committee, the conference. The team operation is popular because it gives everyone a sense of security arising out of responsibility subdivided and shared. However, the value of togetherness can easily be over estimated. While the group may have some utility in discussing objectives or reviewing errors, the group itself cannot think and it cannot create. A dozen frowning faces around the conference table are no substitute for one lonely guy struggling at his type writer or layout pad.

14. Merchandising of advertising is a troublesome chore, which is why it is so often neglected. Too bad, because it should be standard operating procedure always to

merchandise advertising to your own organization, sales staff, distributors, retailers— everyone the campaign is designed to help. Merchandising keeps the important people informed and sold, sustain enthusiasm, augments the impact of the advertising. Don't skip it just because it is an infernal nuisance.

15. No matter how much confidence a supervisor has in his staff, he must always act as if something will go wrong unless he stays on the ball all the time. The secret of getting things done as you want them and at the time you want them is to incessantly "follow through and follow up." Work out your own system-lists, tickler cards, bulletin board or report meetings—but be sure you know what's going on. The better your system, the less you'll need it, which is the ideal state of affairs.

16. Everyone has fleeting ideas at odd moments, on the job and off. Most of us depend on memory to retain these fugitive thoughts until some later and more favorable moment. But being fragile, many of them evaporate and are lost forever. A difficult habit to cultivate but a useful one is to carry a small note book to jot down random ideas when they occur—copy themes, head lines, things to do, items to check up on, etc. Once you get used to noting things down and then remembering to refer to the notes, you'll find the procedure a great help.

17. Which is more important—copy or art? Silly question, but it is fought over all the time. The answer is that both should be so fused and interdependent in the final product that they have only a combined effect— not separate impacts. Still, despite their "separate but equal" status, no known power can keep copy writers from scribbling alternative layouts and art directors from rewriting copy.

18. General advice on the use of humor in advertising: be careful! Most advertising techniques have many degrees of effectiveness, ranging from the acceptable to the terrific. Humorous ads have only two—perfect and impossible. Humor is a ten-strike when it is just right— but the odds against it are tremendous.

19. Short copy or long? The debate has gone on since the first copywriter had his first conference with his first boss. This is a problem that calls for a single, definite, infallible rule that fits all situations: always keep copy short—except when your good judgment tells you to make it long.

20. Frequency and persistence are the secret of success in the use of print media. All too many advertising campaigns in news papers and magazines are too sparse to accomplish their mission. A strong campaign in the one or two best publications will invariably produce better results than the typical across-the-board program, with a long media list but a short insertion schedule. Broadcast media with their 13- and 26-week cycles have the right idea.

21. Twenty years in advertising teach a practitioner many useful things—some basic and some merely technical— but the most important lesson of all is that there can be no end to learning in this business. There is as much to learn in the second twenty years as the first—perhaps more. Nothing in advertising and distribution stands still. New problems constantly call for new solutions; even the old problems demand fresh approaches. Advertising is not like geometry in which a proposition or theorem stands immutable forever. In advertising, yesterday's Q.E.D. may be today's biggest flop. That's why in *any* year the advertising man, neophyte or veteran, must have flexibility, an open mind and, above all, a willingness to pry himself loose from familiar, pet ideas in favor of even better ones.

Edward C. Von Tress

S enior Vice-President and Director of Advertising of Curtis Publishing Company since 1956. Since joining Curtis in 1929, served as Post representative; Manager of Holiday; and as Executive Director of Advertising. Deputy Director, Printing and Publishing Division, WPB, during World War II. Vice-Chairman, MAB Committee of MPA. Vice-Chairman, Advertising Council.

Twenty Things A Sales Executive Has Learned

E.C. Von Tress

First, I made my own list of thirty different things I had learned in my advertising life. Then I asked forty-five experienced men, sales executives and old pros in my company to supply their lists of things they had learned that might help young salesmen in this business. These lists were checked against my own. If any point of mine did not appear repeatedly on the other lists, it was cast aside. The end result is the twenty which follow.

1. KNOW YOUR PRODUCT

Sounds simple and obvious. However, the understanding of all the meanings which a modern magazine has for its readers and advertisers is an exacting study that never ends. It can be an exciting adventure too—this pursuit of knowledge of a product where so many elements are challenging intangibles.

Some brief thoughts: The prosaic side is always with us—the memorizing of facts and figures. We *must* be familiar with *all* the data, from the fine print on the rate card to the recent rounds of research, if we are to handle ourselves with assurance. And a bluff, or a misstatement, or a display of ignorance here, can destroy the confidence of a customer.

Read faithfully every issue of your magazine. Each issue is a brand new product, through which your editors give a new interpretation of their editorial aims and philosophy.

Know your readers and what your magazine means to them. Devote at least one week of the year to depth interviews in the homes of your reader families. They will welcome you, for people love to talk about their favorite magazines. There you will get the gospel and the conviction you need to interpret the special impact and influence of your publication on the lives of its audience.

2. KNOW THE "MARKETING" PROBLEMS AND OBJECTIVES OF YOUR ADVERTISERS

This requirement was an ABC of magazine selling as far back as the twenties, but it is still the rock on which many a pick is broken.

It gets tougher all the time since "marketing" today may include research, product design, packaging, distribution, pricing, merchandising, display, and promotion, as well as the actual advertising. And many of these elements may relate to advertising strategy.

One opportunity is always open to all of us—personal calls on the trade—a laboratory for the study of just about every phase of the marketing of a given product.

The time you spend in the field pays off in many ways:

a) It gives you the knowledge you need for a professional, informed approach to your selling program.

b) Usually you will uncover information that will make you welcome in the offices of account and agency people most important to you. At the least, you'll earn good will through this interest in *their* product.

c) You'll make friendships throughout the distributing channels which may be invaluable.

d) Out of the days you devote to the advertiser's problems can come the ideas on the way your publication can help solve these problems.

So here's the outlet for your ingenuity—your "creativity," as they call it these days. Here is where they separate the marketing professionals from the sellers of space.

3. IN YOUR PENETRATION OF ADVERTISERS AND AGENCIES, MAKE CERTAIN YOU KNOW JUST WHO INFLUENCES DECISIONS AND IN WHAT DEGREE; AND MAKE CERTAIN THAT YOU ALLOCATE YOUR TIME AND EFFORTS ACCORDINGLY

In each case the building of essential contacts is a tailored program—the result of continuing study and planned strategy.

Some suggestions: You *must* get your story to the top echelons—and with the right timing. I know an old pro who says: "The best way to meet the president is an introduction from the vice-president, whom you got to know through the advertising manager— if you earn your way."

Enlist a special champion for your cause—a true believer who will fight for you when the chips are down in the closed sessions.

Keep your pipelines open; win a friend inside who will alert you on timing and tactics.

Know the boys in the "back room"—some day you will need them.

4. KNOW YOUR COMPETITION

Learn the strengths as well as the weaknesses of TV, radio, newspapers, supplements, and billboards, as well as the strengths and weaknesses of competing magazines.

5. KNOW THE CURRENT BUSINESS AND ECONOMIC PICTURE

Naturally the magazine man keeps abreast of advertising trends through the trade press, but his required reading may well include business and financial news.

He wants to be equipped to handle himself among top executives with the poise and confidence of a *well informed* businessman.

6. SALES MANAGE YOURSELF. THERE ARE FEW SALES JOBS WHERE THE SALESMAN IS SO MUCH ON HIS OWN AS IN THE MAGAZINE FIELD.

Remember that time is your most precious asset and that your progress will depend on how profitably you use it.

Analyze your account list regularly, according to relative potential and need for immediate attention.

On each key account make sure that you concentrate your efforts on individuals according to the measure of influence which each man has on advertising decisions.

Have a definite objective for each major account, based on knowledge of its marketing problems and its advertising strategy. Report progress or change regularly to your boss or to *yourself.*

Each of us seeks to make as many calls as possible. The daily struggle is to *get out of the office* for most of the day without neglecting desk work. I have never seen anyone lick this problem unless he scheduled his calls in advance and planned his time for days ahead.

Timing, timing, timing. We *must* be at the right man's desk at the right time. Surely no other element is quite so vital in this business as timing.

7. MAKE EVERY CALL A CONTRIBUTION TO THE OTHER FELLOW THINKING

He has given you his valuable time—but you won't get in again unless you have given him something worth *his* while. Clearly every call is a "custom job" demanding special preparation.

At certain times an aggressive presentation of your sales story may be what he wants, and the harder you hit the more he will respect you.

On other calls you must come up with ideas about *his* business. Whence come such ideas? Each man of course relies on his individual creative ability and resourcefulness. But there is one common source for ideas open to us all—field work in the trade. Again, this emphasis on personal calls, on wholesalers, jobbers and dealers.

Regardless of the nature of the call, it is always possible to find the way to *ask for an order.*

8. REMEMBER THAT THE TEAM PLAYER IS ALWAYS ONE-UP ON THE MAVERICK (AND THE CHANCES ARE THAT HE HAS A LOT MORE FUN)

We can learn from the old pros and we can benefit from helping the younger men.

As for management, well, it usually pays to be patient when you think they are off the beam. If you are really upset over a policy or an incident, here are suggestions: Keep your sense of humor and keep your grievance to yourself until you can talk it through with management.

Never let a persuasive or protesting buyer get you off base on issues involving the policies of your House.

9. PERFECT YOUR FOLLOW THROUGH, BOTH IN SELLING AND IN SERVICING ACCOUNTS

Here is a verbatim quote from an advertiser: "That man really follows through. It seems he just starts to work when he gets an order—he not only keeps on selling but he keeps finding ways to help make the advertising pay off."

This seems to be the kind of operation which really registers. It is, I believe, the refrain played back most frequently when customers want to cheer a salesman's efforts.

10. KEEP FIT

Sooner or later most of us learn that our mental and physical best is barely good enough. The best preparation for the "big call" is a good night's sleep, and really every call is the "big call."

11. AVOID HEAD-ON COLLISIONS

If your man expresses strong convictions against a point you have made, don't try to argue him down. Respect his integrity and his right to a point of view—then tactfully accept your cue to take a new approach.

12. FIND SOMETHING TO LIKE IN EVERY MAN ON YOUR LIST

Resentment and personal enmities are luxuries we can't afford. There are really no "s.o.b.'s" in this business; let's just say that here and there is a personality puzzle we have not yet solved. Let's keep searching for common interests which can lead to understanding and friendship.

13. NEVER MISS AN OPPORTUNITY TO SELL THE VALUES OF MAGAZINES AS A MEDIUM TO MOVE GOODS AND BUILD LASTING GROWTH

14. BE SURE YOU KNOW HOW TO MAKE AN EXIT

Here is the way my first boss, a rugged character, summed up his selling philosophy: "Know what you are talking about; it ain't just what you say—it's how you say it; go after an order like Casanova went for a Venetian blonde; and *when you get the order get the hell out of there.*"

15. SELL CONTINUITY

Keep the pressure on for *adequate* use of your magazine, and you will serve well your advertisers and your publisher.

16. THE COMPETITIVE SPIRIT

The degree that this instinct is inherent in a man's makeup may be a measure of his progress in this business. Perhaps the young salesman, after a few times around the track, might well ask himself these questions: Do I really *hurt* when I lose an order? Do I find my greatest rewards and compensations in the fun and excitement of winning the tough ones? If he cannot answer "yes" to both the questions, he had better take a long look at himself to be sure he is in the right business.

17. CONTAGIOUS ENTHUSIASM

A man may go far through calm persuasion and careful presentation of facts and statistics; but the job is a lot easier when a kind of crusading conviction shines through everything a salesman says. Contagious enthusiasm may be developed, although it must be more than a superficial attitude. It must spring from loyalty to one's company, from an abiding belief in one's product, and from a true understanding of how that product can serve the advertiser.

18. SOME THINGS TO WORRY ABOUT AS WE GROW OLDER

In any field, as a man matures he masters his craft and results come easier. It is only human to fall into dangerous habits of thinking and action. Of the evils which beset us I will presume to name three: *careless 'planning, cynicism, complacency*—and the most deadly of these is complacency.

19. KNOW YOURSELF

Each morning in the mirror the magazine salesman faces his real boss—the one guy who can't be fooled—who knows how much was accomplished the day before and what plans have been made for the day ahead, the week ahead, the month ahead. Why not talk it through each morning with the guy in the mirror?

20. THIS ABOVE ALL: EARN AND CHERISH THE TRUST OF YOUR CUSTOMERS

Without this trust you are dead; with it you are off to a running start.

Selling magazine advertising in a climate of mutual trust and respect can make for a rewarding business life; and it can be a whale of a lot of fun.

Janet Wolff

In a few spectacular years, Janet Wolff has become established as an authority on today's woman. Copy director of an agency before she was twenty-five, she is now Vice President and senior copy group head at the J. Walter Thompson Company. She has helped develop such feminine slanted campaigns as "That Ivory Look," "Nothing Measures Up to Wool," Scotkins "wet strength," and Emily Tipp for the Ward Baking Company. Her book, *What Makes Women Buy,* published by McGraw-Hill and now translated into two foreign languages, reflects her absorbing interest in the problems of selling to women.

Twenty Things I've Learned in Selling to Women

Janet L Wreff

1. *Don't tell everything you know to women* or be a know-it-all. If you close your mind to new ideas, the world and women will leave you far behind.

2. *Women take life—and you and advertising and everything— personally.* Once a woman identifies with an advertisement or a product or a sales message, she automatically becomes personally involved. She sees things only in relation to herself. She thinks: "is it right for me," "would it suit my daughter," "does it fit into my home."

   That's why it's best to approach women on a personal basis. Talk to each woman as an individual—let her know what your product or service can do for *her.*

3. *A woman naturally identifies with the things around her.* She becomes interested in a product or advertisement when she makes this identification—sees something familiar, sees something of herself. If

you've ever noticed a woman window shopping, she'll stroll along glancing in the store windows, then suddenly she'll stop and become extremely attentive—she's noticed her own reflection.

Women are inclined to identify more readily with certain* people than others. Next to her own self, a woman identifies most quickly with another woman. A photograph of a woman in an advertisement will generally catch a woman's eye, gain her attention more quickly than any other person. The more that woman in the picture is like what she would like to be, the more a woman is going to be interested. Most women today picture themselves as, or would like to be ... active, trim, natural-looking (as opposed to overly glamorous) women.

Famous women, babies and children, couples, famous men follow in just about that order for gaining a woman's interest. Family groups and men are much less effective.

Making identification, becoming interested, naturally has nothing to do with feeling a person is authoritative. There are many times when a woman may feel a man carries more authority than a woman. For instance, she often may feel a male announcer on the television knows more about a washing machine or that the recipes of a famous male chef will be better than something a housewife has concocted in the kitchen.

4. *Women like to be participants—not merely spectators.* They want to put something of themselves in every job . . . either for the personal satisfaction they'll get from it or for the thanks and acknowledgment they'll receive from other people.

So, instead of emphasizing what a product can do, it's preferable to play up what a woman can do with the product. By all means make sure that there *is* something for her to do, so she will have a feeling of creating, participating—something which other people will be able to see she has done. A good example of this is found in canned soups. Here was a good product that did it all. A woman just opened the can, heated it and there was a fine soup. Once the novelty of this wore off, the women of a new era began to want to do more. So the soup people have offered today's women ways of being individual and creative by adding garnishes and mixing different kinds of soups.

In the actual selling job, as well as the product itself, leaving room for a woman to participate is essential. Don't tell her everything. Leave something to her imagination. Start her off in the right direction and leave the details for her to fill in. Letting the woman join in has two valuable functions. One, she will remember a lot longer. Two, she will add the personal touch from her own experience herself (that you can't possibly do with every single person) which is often the difference between making a sale and not making a sale.

5. *Women are never happy with the status quo.* They always want to change things, to improve things, to find something new. Newness and change are essential to feminine happiness—"let's rearrange the living room furniture" . . . "perhaps sister needs a new school" . . . "Why don't you try one of those new English tailored suits?"

In buying, women are always on the lookout for something new and different . . . and better. So in selling to women, we can't simply stand pat even with the best product. Next year we have to offer women something new—a fashion color, a better package, extra performance. If we don't, women will seek out the producer who does offer them the new, the different.

6. *A woman's senses are extremely acute.* In buying, she depends on them as her main guide. Each time she considers a purchase all her senses go to work to help her out.

We have to be sure that our product ... and the atmosphere around our product . . . meet all the requirements of her senses, appeal to her senses. In short, the product and the place of sale must be pleasing—look good and feel right and have a pleasant odor or good taste and nice sound.

In addition, women have preconceived notions about the sensory appeal of certain products. For instance, women expect a certain characteristic odor from baby products. When brightly colored bread was tested on the market, women simply wouldn't buy it or claimed it didn't taste good. Good glassware must have the clear ring of a bell. Cleaning powders, shampoos, etc., must make suds. Before new products are marketed, a check should be made to see what preconceived notions there may be ... and to discover women's readiness to accept something different, and plans should be made for overcoming these notions.

7. *Details are extremely important to women.* In fact, women often become so preoccupied with the details of a matter that they miss the overall point.

In selling to women, we must be certain that every detail of the product and the sales message is perfect. Any minor imperfection will be noticed by women . . . will completely capture their attention. When this happens the rest of the sales message is completely lost to them or they discredit the rest of the story, assume it is also inaccurate.

This also works in reverse. When the details are accurately, sensitively done, women will notice and appreciate them. These details may often be the deciding factor in a sale.

8. *Women are creatures with high-key emotions.* They freely show their emotions, are guided in many circumstances by these emotions, act upon their feelings. Most women arrive at decisions by an "intuitive" process rather than factual, logical reasoning. Most often they buy for emotional reasons.

Sales appeal based on emotion is often the most effective. A woman wants to know the "feelings" behind the product rather than just the facts. She is interested in how the product will affect her, what other people think about the product, how the product will help her family.

When a woman gets a "feeling"—good or bad—about a product, all the facts in the world are not likely to change her mind. For her decision was based on emotion and usually only an emotional approach can get her to change her mind.

This is not to say that facts have no place in selling to women. They do—but they are often more effective a sales tool in combination with emotion. When she buys a new chest of drawers for the bedroom she wants to know the dimensions and the material and so on, but naturally the basic reason she wants the chest at all may not be because it has these dimensions.

Facts can also help a woman to reinforce the emotional decisions she has already made. She feels she is doing the right thing when the food she wants and buys is packed with nutritive value or the phonograph is guaranteed unbreakable. And when she arrives home with her purchases, these facts help a woman sell her husband on her decisions.

9. *Women have tangible rather than abstract wants. A* contemporary authority on women once said: Men want a happy home, while women want the things that go to make up a happy home.

Most women's minds do not dwell on the abstract, the intangible. Every problem, every idea, every product is translated by a woman into the terms of her everyday life, her own experience.

Women's attitude toward money is a good case in point. Women see money not as something of value in itself but in terms of what it will buy. If her husband gets a $10 a week raise, a woman immediately translates this into something "actual" like a new refrigerator. Money is useful only when usefully spent. A woman won't put her heart into saving against some general sickness, but she will work at saving for the time Johnny may need an operation or braces on his teeth. She is more apt to save for the vacation in the *mountains* than a vacation "in general."

Selling women intangible services is a difficult job. The most successful way to accomplish it is to translate the service into realistic, tangible terms. Emphasize the benefits, the end results for a woman and her family, rather than dwelling on the method of the service. In recent years, the life insurance people have done a superb job of putting their service into women's terms. And it is important that this translation be done at the personal selling level as well as in advertising.

10. *Talk to women as if they were your intellectual equal.* Women's intellectual capacities and abilities are equal to men's, according to all leading scientific tests. In these tests women show a decidedly superior memory. These statements are not an attempt to start a feminist argument. They are merely recorded because of their importance in selling to women.

In selling, women's equal intelligence simply means that any tendency to talk down to the feminine sex should be carefully avoided. There is apparently no necessity for it, and women are going to heartily resent it. When any mechanical apparatus is involved, there is a decided tendency to be condescending to women. While women do not have great mechanical interest or special ability, they dislike being approached as if they were preschool children. For instance, instead of saying "you don't need mechanical ability to do it," a vacuum cleaner salesman might merely point out that "a push of the button starts the motor."

11. *There is "jive" talk, there is "baby" talk, "bridge" talk, "man-to-man" talk—and there is "woman" talk.* Women have a special way of expressing themselves, of putting their words together, that is all their own. Certain words mean one thing to a woman, another thing to a man. To take just one example: the word "base" is likely to mean "powder base" to a woman and "third base" to a man.

To effectively communicate with women, we must talk their language. The message means something to women, makes contact with women when it is phrased their way. This involves shying away from technical terms and numbers which do not interest women, but often just confuse the issue for them. But more importantly, it means using their exact words and expressions which can only be learned by leaving our desks and going out and talking to them.

12. *Women have a feeling of insecurity.* In tests measuring the attitudes and characteristics of men and women, the greatest difference is found in the degree of confidence. Women as com pared to men show a decided lack of confidence, have a feeling of insecurity.

This feeling has been heightened in the women of this generation because of cultural factors. The woman of today must constantly adapt to rapid and radical changes . . . she lives under the threat of war and destructive inventions ... is faced with "finding herself" in a time when the feminine role is going through a stage of transition. So many of the things about our life today leave a woman wondering what is right and what is wrong, what is the "proper" thing to do. Most women today need to be constantly reassured that what they are doing is right— whether it is as simple a matter as the dress they are wearing or the more complex matter of going to work.

In selling, this has two meanings. First, the product we are selling must radiate confidence and security. Through advertising and packaging and display, we must let women know that this product is safe and "right" and acceptable. Second, through our advertising and products we can give women a feeling of security. This can become a major selling point. The woman who uses the product will *know* she is right, will have confidence in what she is doing.

13. *The family has taken on new significance, has a new form in recent years.* The family group is more important to everyone in the family than it was in the last generation . . . and the emphasis has fallen on the children. The family works together, plays together, plans together. There is every evidence that this trend will continue with full force into the next generation . . . however, with one major difference. In the future it is likely that individual pursuits within the family group will become more important.

The woman of today considers her family first when it comes to buying. Selfish purchases are out . . . each item is considered in the light of how it will affect the entire family. For instance, a new permanent for mother may have to take a back seat to a television set for the whole family. A woman may forego fine, stemmed glassware in favor of tumblers because of the children.

There is hardly a product that cannot be related to the family, and hardly a product that will not benefit from being related to the family. Take clothes for example. Clothes are an individual purchase . . . has immediate benefit only for the wearer. But in the end result they can influence the whole family. "The family is proud of a woman who always looks her best. The best-dressed families get ahead."

This emphasis on the family has also made the selling appeal of being a better wife and mothers a powerful one. The woman of today finds it harder to fulfill the many new demands of managing a family. She looks for help in raising physically and mentally healthy children, in arranging trips and recreation for the whole family group, in contributing to her husband's job, in handling the family car, in managing the family finances—in all the new things she is called upon to do. If our products can make the doing easier or better, we have a strong selling point which should be emphasized.

14. *Psychology has been 'popularized in the last several decades.* "Complex," "traumatic experience," "neurosis" have become every-day words for women. Women have been fascinated with the subject of psychology for they have always had an inward turn of mind—always been preoccupied with what people think and feel. Psychology has also added to women's insecurities— for a great deal of time has been spent in analyzing modern women and their modern responsibilities. As more answers come from this speculation in the future there will probably be less fear and insecurity on women's part—but the interest promises to continue.

Psychology not only makes for good reading in magazines, but is an excellent way to capture a woman's interest in advertisement and in selling to her. If your product has a possible psychological twist, dig it out and tell women about it—it can be most effective.

15. *Today's women are both 'phased and displeased by a phenomenon hest termed "instant living."* Appliances, packaged foods, fabulous fabrics and the like have taken a great deal of the backbreaking labor out of women's lives—for which they are appreciative. The "miracle of convenience" captured women's attention and fancy completely after World War II. Today they still want convenience . . . but actually expect to get it in everything they buy as a matter of course. So, built-in convenience in products is as necessary as ever, but today seldom important enough to be *the* major selling point.

Women have also become somewhat disenchanted with "instant living," for various reasons. One reason is that the miracles have not made life that much easier, for new standards have also been added. Washing machines mean washing more often, wash-and-wear suits mean work at home instead of sending them to the cleaner, vacuum cleaners mean cleaning the house more often.

Another thing women have discovered about "instant living" is that it takes some of the fun, much of the creativity out of homemaking. Many tasks seem routine. An excellent supper can be had from a package . . . without even dirtying a pan. This feeling of not contributing is a factor in the recent rise in gourmet cooking.

So if we have a product to sell that gives a woman an opportunity to be creative—or saves her time so that she may spend her hours in more creative fashion—we surely should play it up as a big factor.

16. *Today there are no set roles for men and women.* Wives go out to work, husbands help around the house. Most women are not sure what is their responsibility and what is their husband's.

The women of today are looking for guides—trying to establish a new pattern of living. In selling to them, we can help establish guides—tell them how successful women manage and arrange their lives. And we must be sure that our products become a part of the new pattern that is emerging. Our products have to fit into the life of a modern woman whose scope is broadening to include the world as well as her own backyard.

As part of the changing roles of the sexes, an attitude has grown up that "merely being a housewife" is not enough. How or why this feeling has developed is not the question here. What is important is that most women feel being a housewife is a singularly unglamorous and unappreciated job—and that their family and friends feel it is not a full-time job. The homemaker is in need of a little promotion and ego building, and those of us in selling are in a position to give it to her. We can tell her that she is necessary, that she is doing a good job— especially if she uses our product. As long as we do so sincerely, she will give us her undivided attention.

17. *Today's women are "mobiles."* They are busy moving from one house to another, from one community to another, from one section of the country to another. Once every five years the equivalent of the entire population moves—this is quite a contrast to the past, even the recent past. In addition to physically moving about, women are also busy moving from one social group to another—this is perhaps the more exhausting task.

The importance of strong brands and brand images in a mobile society such as this can hardly be overstated.

When a woman makes a move with her family from one coast to another, the only familiar thing in her life may well be the brands on the supermarket shelf. Get a woman to know your brand and she will take it with her wherever she goes, as a friend. In the past, a woman could turn to the friends in her community for help. Often today, brands, reliable brands, must serve the same function.

Certain types of products and brands also become associated with people who live in a certain manner. As women move up the social scale they will look to these products. For instance, Bermuda shorts for women and sport shirts for men have become popular due to suburbia. As new families move into the suburbs, they are suddenly in the market for these products. It is necessary to develop a strong association between your product and a certain type of person or manner of living. If the brand image is weak, then it is likely that no one will be interested.

18. *Women need help to meet exacting standards.* While the entire rules of living are in flux, women today find themselves under pressure to meet exacting standards of a general type. To be a good wife and mother, for instance, a woman must be attractive, well mannered, well dressed . . . have a happy family, well adjusted children, a successful husband . . . run a well organized household, provide good meals, entertain easily and gracefully. She may also be expected to go to work and help with the family finances. There are other standards and pressures dictated by the community she lives in.

Through our products and sales stories we can help a woman meet these rigorous standards. This is the obvious. But we will find even greater reception if we can show a woman how to relax the standards a little— ease the tensions for her.

19. *Today's woman has a new attitude.* The women—and men— of today have developed a new attitude toward the pleasures of life. The Puritan idea of "all pleasure is sinful" is slowly passing from the American make-up. Today's women feel that they— and their families— should enjoy life now, as they live it. It is not, however, a completely hedonistic attitude of everything for today and nothing for tomorrow. It is more a let's-enjoy-life-*today-and-tomorrow* attitude . . . for women are saving as well as spending.

   Having fun today has become a legitimate and successful sales appeal—which it has not been in the past. But if we are going to make this appeal, we also have to give women some way to get it—that is, credit and service. Both credit and service are becoming essential to the selling job—as essential as built-in convenience is in products.

20. *Each woman is a distinct and separate individual made up of many parts.* This is one of the important things to remember in selling to women—especially when not selling person to person.

   She is first of all a woman which gives her specific and special characteristics—some of which we have briefly covered. She has to be approached as a woman—in a far different manner than when selling a man.

   She is also a member of a distinct community group. She has ideas that come from being identified with this group. Polka dots are good in California but not in Maine. In the South women need narrower shoes than women in the East. To sell women effectively, the many community differences must be noted and taken into account.

   Wherever she lives, she belongs to a certain age group (teenage or middle age or older) and a certain kind of working group (married or single, working at home, working outside the home). It is next to impossible to appeal to all of these groups of women at once. A group must be singled out and the sales message aimed in that direction.

Last of all, each woman is a distinct and separate individual with problems and ideas and wants all her own. We must get through to her as that individual, answer her individual problems and wants to sell her. She doesn't want what thousands of other women want. She wants what suits her, what pleases her—what makes her different from any one else in the world.

CPSIA information can be obtained at www.ICGtesting.com
Printed in the USA
BVOW02s1047130913

331120BV00001B/33/P